Handwriting OF THE Famous AND Infamous

HANDWRITING OF THE FAMOUS AND INFAMOUS

Sheila Lowe

MetroBooks

MetroBooks

An Imprint of Friedman/Fairfax Publishers

This edition published by Metrobooks by arrangement with Brown Partworks Limited.

ISBN 1-58663-226-4

Printed and bound in Singapore

Project Editor: Jane Lanigan
Design: Brown Partworks
Picture Research: Susannah Jayes and Gemma Brockis

Important note

Just as someone's personality may change over time, so too can their handwriting. According to the writer's reaction to various external factors, such as a death in the family, separation or divorce, health problems, a job change, or some kind of physical trauma, their handwriting may undergo alterations that may or may not be permanent. Some medications, as well as alcohol and recreational drugs, can also have a temporary or a lasting effect on a person's writing and so can potentially affect the results of the handwriting analysis to some degree.

Many of the samples in *Handwriting of the Famous and Infamous* are undated, so we do not know the age of the person at the time of writing or the circumstances under which he or she wrote. In some cases the dates show that the writing was done when the writer was under great stress. Stalin's handwriting sample, for instance, is dated three months into the invasion of the Soviet Union by Germany, when he was under enormous pressure.

Introduction

Research tells us that every experience we ever have is stored in the brain. When one begins to write, the unconscious reaction to those experiences is left in the trail of ink. Thus, handwriting can properly be termed brainwriting.

The study of handwriting is called graphology–from the Greek words *graphein* (to write) and *logos* (study of). Graphology is based on common sense, not hocus pocus. For instance, a messy, disorganized handwriting reflects a writer who is likely to be sloppy in the way they look, leave their bed unmade, and so on. And handwriting is a lot like body language. A friendly, outgoing person may lean forward enthusiastically to shake your hand. He probably has right-slanted writing. A more reserved person writes with an upright slant. It takes a combination of art and science to produce an accurate picture of personality by analyzing one's handwriting.

Graphology has been around for hundreds of years, with one of the earliest references made to the handwriting of Augustus Caesar. Closer to modern times, in the late 1800s a French monk named Abbe Michon categorized handwriting by its individual strokes, which he linked to specific personality traits. Others later preferred to interpret handwriting as a whole entity, making inferences about personality through the overall arrangement on the page. Widely used in Europe and taught in universities there until World War II, graphology went underground when Hitler outlawed most systems of study. It is currently enjoying an international resurgence of popularity.

Some of the many applications of handwriting analysis include personality assessment for hiring and counseling employees; relationship compatibility; helping parents understand their children and vice-versa; and, of course, helping people understand themselves better, too. There's even a branch of handwriting analysis called graphotherapy, which teaches handwriting exercises to help change personality traits.

Handwriting cannot reveal everything—personality is too complex for that. But it does unmask many important aspects of how the writer thinks, feels, and acts. The portrait it paints of personality is truly a reflection of who the writer is inside.

Sheila Lowe

Key to profession titles

 Politician   Showmanship   Genius   Adventure   Strength

 Creative   Morality   Monarchy   Money   Military

Contents

Jane Austen   6–7

Johann Sebastian Bach   8–9

Ludwig van Beethoven   10–11

David Berkowitz   12–13

Ted Bundy   14–15

George Bush, Sr.   16–17

George W. Bush, Jr.   18–19

Lord Byron   20–21

Andrew Carnegie   22–23

Fidel Castro   24–25

Catherine the Great   26–27

Charlie Chaplin   28–29

Winston Churchill   30–31

Bill Clinton   32–33

Hillary Clinton   34–35

Kurt Cobain   36–37

Christopher Columbus   38–39

Marie Curie   40–41

George Custer   42–43

Charles Darwin   44–45

James Dean   46–47

Princess Diana   48–49

Charles Dickens   50–51

Emily Dickinson   52–53

Amelia Earhart   54–55

Thomas Edison   56–57

Albert Einstein   58–59

Elizabeth I   60–61

Duke Ellington   62–63

William Faulkner   64–65

F. Scott Fitzgerald   66–67

Benjamin Franklin   68–69

Sigmund Freud   70–71

Galileo Galilei   72–73

Ulysses S. Grant   74–75

John Hancock   76–77

Ernest Hemingway   78–79

Jimi Hendrix   80–81

Henry VIII   82–83

Adolf Hitler   84–85

Thomas Jefferson   86–87

Jacqueline Kennedy Onassis   88–89

John F. Kennedy   90–91

Robert E. Lee   92–93

John Lennon   94–95

Leonardo da Vinci   96–97

Abraham Lincoln   98–99

Louis XIV   100–101

Paul McCartney   102–103

Margaret Mitchell   104–105

James Monroe   106–107

Marilyn Monroe   108–109

Wolfgang Amadeus Mozart   110–111

Napoleon Bonaparte   112–113

Lee Harvey Oswald   114–115

George Patton   116–117

Edgar Allan Poe   118–119

Jackson Pollock   120–121

Elvis Presley   122–123

Ronald Reagan   124–125

John D. Rockefeller   126–127

Eleanor Roosevelt   128–129

Franklin D. Roosevelt   130–131

Ernest Shackleton   132–133

O. J. Simpson   134–135

Joseph Stalin   136–137

Mother Teresa   138–139

Dylan Thomas   140–141

Donald Trump   142–143

Queen Victoria   144–145

George Washington   146–147

James Whistler   148–149

Oscar Wilde   150–151

Virginia Woolf   152–153

Wilbur Wright   154–155

Jane Austen

English Novelist (1775–1817)

Jane Austen was born in Hampshire, England, the seventh of eight children. Her father was a scholarly man who encouraged learning in his children, while her mother was well known for her wit and stories. Austen began writing around 1787 and over the next five years filled three manuscript notebooks with her stories and prose. Her first novel, *Sense and Sensibility,* was published anonymously in 1811, followed two years later by *Pride and Prejudice.* The works were well received, and were highly favored by then Prince Regent (later George IV). Austen is often credited with having given the novel its modern character, dealing as she did with ordinary people and their inner lives.

Personality overview

The large, round middle-zone writing that can usually be seen in modern young women of Austen's time is missing. In its place we find a well-organized writing with a focus on movement, with narrow margins, a strong right slant, and long lower zone. At the time of writing Austen was probably an active young woman, easily bored, whose interests encompassed a wide range.

Relationships

The writing has expanded spaces between letters, but the letters themselves are narrow, which suggests that Austen was a bit shy. Nonetheless, underneath that calm, pleasant demeanor was the lively, fun-loving spirit of someone whose restlessness could soon turn into frustration without the right outlet. The right slant and high degree of connectedness between letters shows that she was a good friend who could be counted on for a listening ear when it was needed.

Intellectual forces

Austen had a quick wit, as seen in the long *t*-crosses, tall upper zone, and missing initial strokes. She had an intellectual bent, and would thoroughly investigate anything that caught her fancy. She adopted the Greek *d*, which is often referred to as the poet's *d*, and is viewed as a sign of one who is good at writing—no surprise in this instance.

Physical drives

Emotional and affectionate, Austen's pastose writing shows a love for nature and all things beautiful. With the extra-long lower zone we can be sure that she kept many irons in the fire, was always active and ready for adventure. For the same reason, her judgments would tend to be based on instinct, but since the upper zone is also well developed, she would be able to balance her gut reactions with principle.

Motivating forces

The tall, narrow upper zone, well-formed capital letters, and thick strokes indicate someone who derived a sense of honor from the values that she learned from her parents. She had a strong conscience and, committed to seeing beauty and good in others, would be willing to make great sacrifices for what she believed in.

Between the lines

The lower zone encompasses the area below the baseline, including lower loops and any parts of letters that fall into that area. It is in this zone that the instinctual, biological urges reside, and it reflects the strength of the writer's need and desire for food, sex, money, and material goods. A long lower zone generally means a busy person, as in Austen's case. The writer's attitudes toward the past, his or her mother, wishes and dreams, are also found in the lower zone.

GreenPark 13ʰ. Monday Janᵞ 21ˢᵗ. —

My dearest Frank

I have melancholy news to relate, & sincerely feel for your feelings under the shock of it. — I wish I could better prepare You for it — But having said so much, Your mind will already foretell the sort of Event which I have to communicate. — Our dear Father has closed his virtuous & happy life, in a death almost as free from suffering as his Children could have wished. — He was taken ill on Saturday morning, exactly in the same way as heretofore, an oppression in the head, with fever, violent tremulousness, & the greatest degree of Feebleness. The same remedy of Cup=ping, which had before been so Successful, was imme=diately applied to — but without such happy effects.

Extract from a letter written by Jane Austen to her brother in 1805

GreenPark... Monday January 21st

My dearest Frank
I have melancholy news to relate, & sincerely feel for your feelings under the shock of it. I wish I could better prepare you for it —But having said so much, your mind will already foretell the sort of event which I have to communicate.—Our dear father has closed his virtuous and happy life, in a death almost as free from suffering as his Children could have wished. He was taken ill on Saturday morning, exactly in the same way as heretofore, an oppression in the head with fever, violent tremulousness (?), and the greatest degree of feebleness. The same remedy of cupping which had before been so successful, was immediately applied to—but without such happy effects....

Johann Sebastian Bach

GERMAN MUSICIAN, COMPOSER (1685–1750)

Chiefly recognized by his contemporaries as a talented organist, Bach spent his career as a church musician and composer in relatively obscure German towns. The vast body of sacred and secular music he produced, however, displays a creativity and mastery of musical theory that make him one of the greatest of all composers and an influence on successive generations from Haydn and Mozart to Arnold Schoenberg.

Personality overview

Bach's handwriting gives the impression of an eager, impatient person who can hardly wait to get on with the next project. The speedy, simplified forms and decreasing right margins are indicative of a desire to move forward. The emphasis is on movement and the rhythm is strong but disturbed. Bach needed to stay busy, but was not always entirely consistent in how he produced results.

Relationships

Except for the broad upper margin, the picture of space is crowded in the beginning, but expands the further Bach moves down the page. We might construe this as initial caution that later gives way to increased passionate excitement and less self-restraint. The combined threads and angles indicate Bach's ability to communicate with many different types of people, making appropriate adjustments according to whomever he was talking to, whether it was a servant or a king.

Intellectual forces

Bach's writing is filled with elaborate forms and ballet-like leaps into the upper zone. His imagination was at work full time, constantly pressing him to create. The thready connective forms are a component of speed, which, in turn, is a sign of intelligence. Sometimes he wrote so fast that legibility suffered as a result.

Physical drives

The crowded words and lines suggest someone who worked in bursts of energy, with a long spell of activity being followed by a slack period. The pressure appears to be fairly light, which is another indicator of a person whose stamina is not long-lasting. Bach could expend a great deal of energy over a limited period but then, when the work was done, would be totally exhausted.

Motivating forces

As is to be expected, the impetus to create seems to dominate Bach's handwriting. He expends much of his energy in the upper zone, where imagination and creativity find an outlet. Here there are large circles, accents, and emphasized capital letters. The material world of the middle and lower zones is de-emphasized by comparison, and the pressure is not strong. For Bach the emphasis was far more on the spiritual side of life.

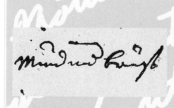

Between the lines

Today circle i-dots are generally adopted by two categories of writers: the creative type (for instance, if the circles in Bach's script are i-dots, then they represent imagination), and the immature writer who wishes to draw attention to him or herself. A small, round dot placed close to the stem of the i suggests a careful, detail-oriented person, while a dot formed more like a dash may signify impatience.

A poem written by Bach, probably to his wife Anna Magdalena

Your servant, sweetest maiden bride:
Joy be with you this morning!
To see you in your flowery crown
And wedding-day adorning
Would fill with joy the sternest soul.
What wonder, as I meet you,
That my fond heart and loving lips
O'erflow with song to greet you.

Ludwig van Beethoven

GERMAN COMPOSER (1770–1827)

Born in Bonn, Germany, Ludwig van Beethoven became a professional musician at 11 years of age, studying with both Mozart and Haydn in Vienna, Austria. Emotional and scruffy in person, he wrote music in all forms that reached new depths of emotional expression and presaged the romantic movement. Famously afflicted with deafness toward the end of his life, he also suffered emotional problems and composed little during the 1820s.

Personality overview

Beethoven's handwriting has the same restless quality as his musical scores. Although the rhythm is disturbed, there is obvious intelligence in the simplification, originality, and expressiveness of the forms. At the same time, legibility is to some degree impaired, revealing impatience and frustration. The variable size of the middle zone depicts a person whose sense of self-worth fluctuated a great deal, from self-assurance and confidence to feelings of inadequacy, often within a very short period of time.

Relationships

Beethoven was extremely sensitive and his moodiness, as seen in the variability along the baseline, would have made him very difficult to live with. Wrapped up in his emotions, he was careless of how he treated others. When he was feeling upbeat, he could undoubtedly be quite charming, but as doubts crept in his self-confidence would suffer to the degree that he felt worthless. Certainly, his highs were very high, as can be seen in the wild leaps into the upper zone. However, he could just as easily plunge into depression.

Intellectual forces

Despite his emotional nature, Beethoven's writing shows fairly good line and word spacing, although there is some zonal interference between the lines. There is also a sense of moving upward, with diagonal strokes thrusting into the "stratosphere" of the writing field—clearly Beethoven's aspirations took him to great heights. However, many of the *i*-dots are made as dashes, a sign of irritability and impatience.

Physical drives

In some areas, the lower zone drops too close to the line below, sometimes interfering with the letters in the next line. This shows a lack of good judgment in the way Beethoven used his resources, that he did not fully recognize what was important and what was not. His extravagance can be seen in rhythm, the writing appearing released (loose) rather than contracted.

Motivating forces

The writing is done at great velocity, with unformed letters and scarce attention to detail. Just looking at the nervous, jumpy script gives one a sense of the torment.

Between the lines

Hooks or tics in handwriting may be large or so small that it takes a magnifying lens to see them. Where they occur at the beginnings of words and on *i*-dots, as in Beethoven's script, hooks and tics are the result of speed and show impatience in the writer. Where they occur at the ends of words they signify tenacity. When they appear in the lower zone they are called cradles and signify emotional insecurity.

An extract from one of Beethoven's letters to the "Immortal Beloved"

This letter was written over two days, July 6 and 7, in 1812.

July 6th, in the morning

 My angel, my all, my very self—only a few words today, and, what is more, writen in pencil (and with your pencil)—I shan't be certain of my rooms here until tomorrow; what an unnecessary waste of time is all this—Why this profound sorrow, when necessity speaks—can our love endure without sacrifices, without our demanding everything from one another; can you alter the fact that you are not wholly mine, that I am not wholly yours?—Dear God …

David Berkowitz

SERIAL KILLER – "SON OF SAM" (1953–   )

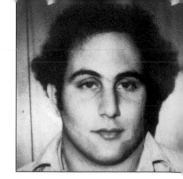

David Berkowitz was born in New York, the result of an illicit affair. When his father forced his mother to give him up, he was adopted by a couple who doted on him. Although Berkowitz was always something of a loner, the death of his adopted mother when he was 12 years of age was a devastating experience for him. He began to withdraw all the more and to indulge in schizophrenic fantasies. In 1976 he went on a 13-month killing spree in New York City that resulted in the deaths of six people, and serious injuries to seven others. Berkowitz is currently serving 365 years in Attica penitentiary.

Personality overview

The handwriting is unremarkable, as many serial killer's scripts are. That is why they are able to fit in with society so easily and are hard to catch. They seem like anyone you might meet on the street. Berkowitz's is a weak writing with a fluctuating slant and light pressure. It reveals a poorly developed ego in a person whose inner drives leave him in emotional turmoil.

Relationships

The softness of the handwriting, along with the weak, often shaky, rightward-tending lower zone, are hallmarks of someone who is not entirely comfortable in personal relationships. The rightward pull of the lower zone is moving away from women and against men, so he is not comfortable with either sex. Some lower loops are small and cramped, and few return to the baseline, a sign of a loner. Yet, the back and forth movement indicates that he would be willing to make sacrifices to make a relationship work, if he found someone he felt accepted him.

Intellectual forces

Berkowitz is not unintelligent. The most notable aspect of this handwriting is the overelaboration in the upper zone, in the form of extra-tall, extra-wide loops, which reflects unrealistic fantasy thinking. When he makes a *th* combination, the *t* is much smaller, which is interpreted as a poor self-image. The *t* is seen as a letter that represents oneself in handwriting and, when it is made smaller than other upper-zone letters, such as the *h*, it suggests the writer feels small and inferior.

Physical drives

Rigid initial strokes on several letters are a reminder of Berkowitz's resentment at past slights, both real or imagined. While the lower zone is long, the pressure seems light. The lower zone is also left open, pointing to a lack of emotional fulfillment.

Motivating forces

The variable slant reveals a victim of mixed feelings who suffers a conflict between his mind and his heart. He does not know what he wants. Thus, his motivations depend on the flavor of the month and change haphazardly. It should be noted that prison doctors diagnosed Berkowitz as being paranoid schizophrenic, and his handwriting at the time of the killings was vastly different from current samples.

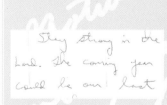

Between the lines

Most handwriting models in schools add strokes to the beginnings of letters as an extra support when a child is learning to write. When initial strokes are retained after graphic maturity is reached, it suggests that the writer needs emotional support from past acquaintances. There are several different types of initial strokes. Curved ones indicate a friendly connection to the past, while rigid, straight ones as in Berkowitz's script attest to resentful feelings and old grudges.

Nov. 18, 1998

Dear Brother

Our days are numbered and the only days that will count are the days we devoted to Jesus Christ. Jesus wants your heart. Give your heart to Him.

Stay strong in the Lord. The coming year could be our last one of this planet.

Happy Thanksgiving!

May His love,
joy, and peace...
all the things that
make Christmas wonderful...
be yours today
and always!

Merry christmas, brother!
Jesus Is Coming Soon!

Your Friend + Bro
David

"Then the angel said to them, 'Do not be afraid, for behold,
I bring you good tidings of great joy which will be to all people.'"
Luke 2:10 NKJV

A Thanksgiving note and a Christmas card from Berkowitz to a friend

Dear Brother
Our days are numbered and the only days that will count are the days we devoted to Jesus Christ. Jesus wants your <u>heart</u>. Give your heart to Him.
Stay strong in the head. The coming year could be our last one of this planet.
Happy Thanksgiving!

Merry Christmas brother!
Jesus Is Coming Soon!
Your friend and Bro.
David

Ted Bundy

AMERICAN SERIAL KILLER (1946–1989)

Ted Bundy, who was born in Vermont, grew up thinking his mother was his sister, a pretense created by her family so she could avoid the shame of being an unmarried mother. Good-looking, intelligent and charismatic, Bundy worked on a suicide hotline, studied psychology and went to law school. However, from around the end of 1973 Bundy had a secret life: he stalked and murdered at least 30 young women in a variety of horrific ways. Eventually one of his intended victims got away and later identified him. Bundy blamed pornography for his crimes and was executed in the electric chair.

Personality overview

The first aspect of Bundy's handwriting to catch the eye is the excessively long, rigid, hooked initial strokes, called harpoons, which begin in the lower zone. Although they are found throughout the writing, they are especially prominent on the left margin, denoting anger and resentment toward past events. The slack, disturbed rhythm, which is often a feature of a criminal's handwriting, signifies a poorly integrated personality. The crowded spatial arrangement of the sample is also indicative of Bundy's inability to keep a clear perspective on his life and to understand what was appropriate behavior in any given situation.

Relationships

The changeable word spacing and variable middle-zone widths show inconsistency in interactions with others. The harpoons, coming from the lower zone where they do not belong, suggest holding on to past slights, be they real or imagined. These harpoons are hidden at first, then shoot up angrily into the middle zone. The many tremulous lower zone strokes reveal Bundy's discomfort in this area of sexual activity. In addition, the overblown personal pronoun, I, has a heavy emphasis on the mother area of the upper loop, so his view of women was not

only unrealistic, but had no father figure to balance it. This skewed view of men and women had to impact on his personal relationships.

Intellectual forces

The upper zone is retraced, denoting a narrow-minded outlook. For Bundy there was no room for anything different or new, this view being supported by the initial strokes beginning in the lower zone, which symbolizes the past. He was stuck with what he had learned early on in life and was too insecure to broaden his outlook.

Physical drives

The long, full lower zone indicates strong drives, yet the rhythm of movement is slack. That is, Bundy had plenty of energy that needed an outlet, but he did not have the drive to do anything consistently positive with it.

Motivating forces

The crowded picture of space, large personal pronoun, and rigid initial strokes suggest a need for power and control. There is not the kind of elastic rhythm that attests to positive energy and willingness to work hard for what he wanted, so Bundy would take control in whatever way was easiest for him at that moment.

Between the lines

When extremely rigid initial strokes are retained in handwriting, they are often a sign of a quarrelsome, contentious person who sees him or herself as a victim of exploitation. The longer and more rigid the stroke, the greater the sense of resentment the writer feels. When the strokes start well into the lower zone, as they do in Bundy's writing, his or her anger and frustration started early in childhood.

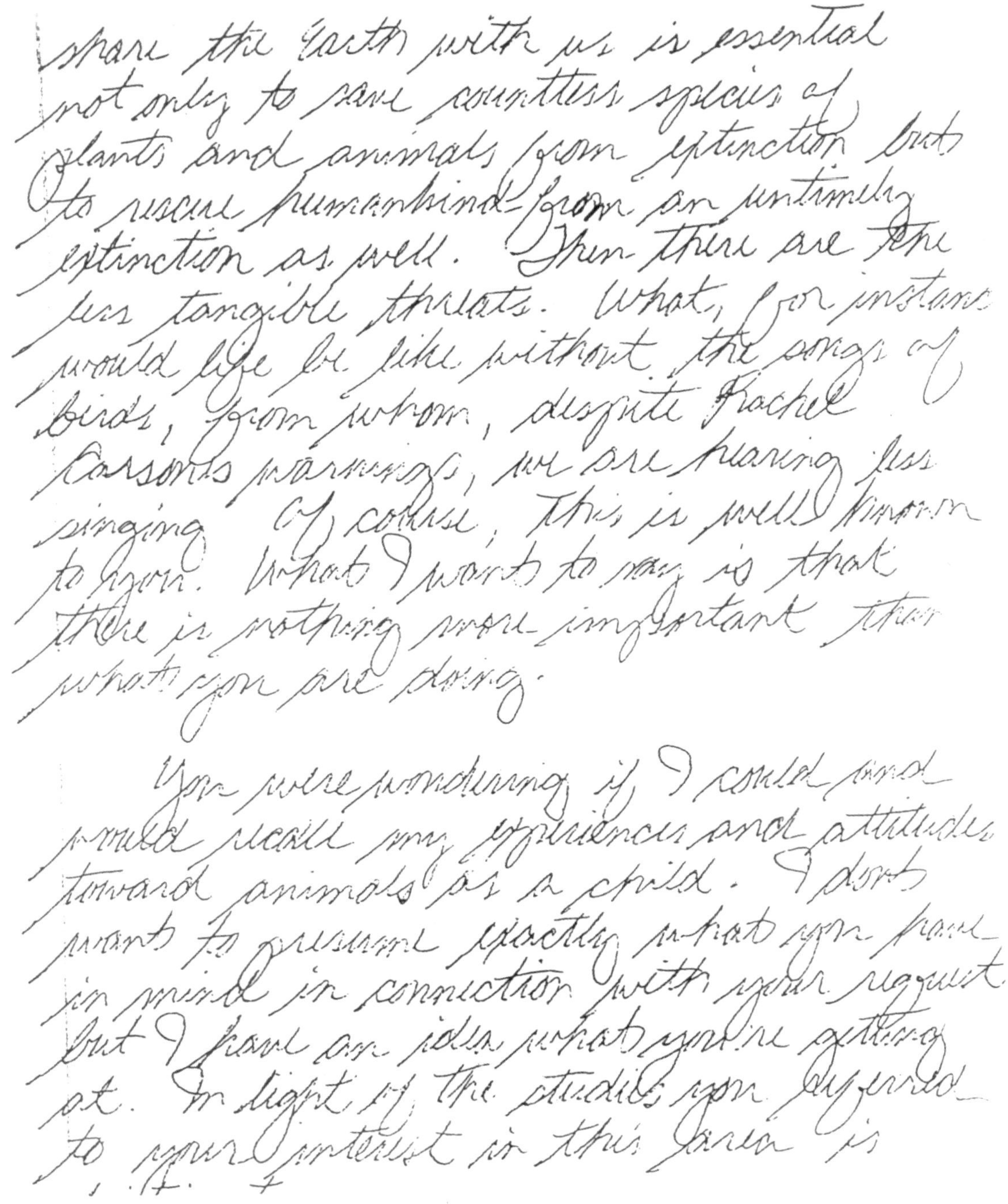

[handwritten letter reproduced below in print]

Extract from a letter (?)written by Ted Bundy

... share the Earth with us is essential not only to save countless species of plants and animals from extinction but to rescue humankind from an untimely extinction as well. Then there are the less tangible threats. What, for instance, would life be like without the songs of birds, from whom, despite Rachel Carson's warnings, we are hearing less singing. Of course, this is well known to you. What I want to say is that there is nothing more important than what you are doing.

You were wondering if I could and would recall my experiences and attitudes toward animals as a child. I don't want to presume exactly what you have in mind in connection with your request but I have an idea what you're getting at. In light of the studies you referred (?) to your interest in this area is ...

George Bush Sr.

41st U.S. President (1924–   )

George Herbert Walker Bush is probably best known as the president who took on Saddam Hussein and Iraq in the Persian Gulf War in 1991. Born in Massachusetts, he enlisted in the Navy and flew dozens of combat missions in World War II, winning the Distinguished Flying Cross. On returning to civilian life, Bush attended Yale University and began his career in the Texas oil industry. In 1959 he became active in the Republican Party and his involvement in politics eventually led to a vice-presidency with Ronald Reagan and, in 1988, a successful bid for the presidency. In 1992 Bush campaigned for reelection, but lost to Bill Clinton.

Personality overview

This is simplified writing with some original forms. The strongly independent personal pronoun, *I*, is made by one who has the self-esteem to live up to his own expectations, rather than following the dictates of others. Yet while Bush has an original approach that allows him to find creative ways of dealing with situations, the rhythm is made choppy by many abrupt starts and stops, showing that he is not entirely comfortable in his own skin.

Relationships

Moodiness is a strong element and a relationship with Bush could be a minefield—people would never know quite what to expect. The variable word spacing suggests that at times he seeks closeness, while at others pushes it away. One moment he is warm and affectionate, the next he might be cool and distant, or irritable and abrupt, depending on his mood. With so many breaks between letters and changes in form, Bush might react one way to a particular situation and quite differently the next time the same situation occurs.

Intellectual forces

Garland connections show a quick thinker whose mind leaps around from one thing to another. Bush relies on first impressions and finds it natural to tap into his intuition to rapidly evaluate people and situations. A strong belief in his gut reactions, even when the evidence does not seem to support his intuitive response, sometimes prompts him to jump to conclusions that may not be correct.

Physical drives

Bush's writing, with its mixture of forms—printing and cursive—as well as the abrupt disconnections between letters and variable spaces between words, indicates a restlessness that makes it hard for him to relax. It is likely that some part of his body is always on the move and tics in the lower zone suggest irritability when he is thwarted in his need for activity. The lack of a return to the baseline also indicates Bush's difficulty in satisfying some of his basic physical needs.

Motivating forces

There are no initial strokes, so Bush is the type of person who takes the initiative—he observes a situation, assesses what needs to be done to take it to the next level, and proceeds accordingly. The high number of angles and tall capitals reflect a need to be in charge and direct affairs, rather than to follow orders.

Between the lines

When the lower zone is abruptly curtailed with a sharp tic, as it is in George H. Bush's script, it suggests irritability and frustration in the most basic of drives. As the lower zone relates to survival instincts—the need for food, sex, money, physical activity, and so on—it can be inferred that some aspect of that area is being left unsatisfied. The urge may be deliberately cut off or there may be a physical cause.

8-31-82

Dear Doro —
   Tomorrow is our big
day. I wish I could
tell you how very much I
love you - You have
given me so much
happiness. Everything
you have done has given
me joy - I love you very
much. That you will
be totally happy with
Billy crowns it all —
   Good night, Pepper —
   Devotedly, Dad —

A letter written by George Bush Sr. to his daughter Dorothy

8.31.82
Dear Doro
   Tomorrow is _our_ big day. I wish I could tell you how very much I love you—You have given me so much happiness.
Everything you have done has given me joy—I love you very much. That you will be totally happy with Billy crowns it all—
   Good night, Pepper—
   Devotedly, Dad—

George W. Bush Jr.

43RD U.S. PRESIDENT (1946–   )

George Walker Bush Jr. received a bachelor's degree at Yale and an MBA at Harvard, and served as a pilot in the Air National Guard. During his career in the oil and gas industry, Bush earned a reputation as a heavy drinker and was responsible for numerous business failures. Later he worked on his father's presidential campaign and became managing partner of the Texas Rangers baseball club. He gave up drink and turned his life around. He was twice elected governor of Texas then, in 2000, his brand of "compassionate conservatism" saw him win a disputed presidential election.

Personality overview

Bush's handwriting is fast and highly simplified in a fairly well-organized writing field. There is some extravagance, as seen in the wide margins and extra-wide word spacing. Also, many indefinite forms lead to illegibility. While his intelligence is obvious, this is someone who takes the easy route wherever possible, rushing ahead without fully considering the outcome of his actions. The tall upper loops signify pride in his achievements, yet, interestingly, his personal pronoun, *I*, is incomplete. The lower loop, representing the father figure, is missing, so Bush does not feel his father was there for him as he was growing up.

Relationships

There is an affable, congenial flow in the thready forms and rightward slant. However, the wide spaces between words and the illegibility tell another story. Bush keeps much to himself and reveals little of his personal side. The signature is quite illegible (as well as being very similar to his father's), which indicates a need for privacy.

Intellectual forces

The simplified forms reveal two things—an ability to strip away extraneous details and get down to basics, and a dislike for detail. Many letters fade out as Bush hurries to get his message down on paper, and there are numerous breaks at inappropriate places. Thoughts are rushing into his head faster than he can express them, and he is too impatient to take the time to clearly explain what he means. He goes with his gut reactions.

Physical drives

Although the lower-zone forms are somewhat variable, the long length and moderate width suggest strong drives and ambitions. The restless quality of the sample reflects a need for action and adventure, while the baseline is somewhat wavy, making adaptability an important key to Bush's success. The changeable writing form, from writing to printing and back again, is indicative of potential difficulties he might have in dealing with high-stress situations.

Motivating forces

The excessively large capital letters in his signature show Bush's "larger-than-life" self image. He sees himself as a star, yet when we look at the body of the writing there is not a great deal of dynamic energy. Some *t*-crosses are strong, while others are rather weak. This shows fluctuations in his goal-directedness.

Between the lines

The width of the middle-zone letters reveals how eager the writer is to satisfy the needs of his or her ego. Oval letters that are nearly as wide as they are tall show the writer actively moves forward and takes what he or she feels is deserved. Narrow or retraced letters show anxiety, which can hamper progress. Bush has average ego needs but a narrow middle zone shows he is not always able to ask for what he wants.

GEORGE W. BUSH

11.23.99

Alan,

I understand that you have volunteered for my campaign. I am grateful to have you on my team.

Your state is very important to winning back the White House. I am working hard to build a strong grassroots organization to carry MI.

I hope you will continue working hard. Together, I am confident we will win.

Sincerely,

George Bush

POST OFFICE BOX 1902, AUSTIN, TEXAS 78767 PHONE 512/637-2000 FAX 512/637-8800 WWW.GEORGEWBUSH.COM

NOT PRINTED OR MAILED AT TAXPAYER EXPENSE

George W. Bush writes to a supporter before the 2000 election campaign

11.23.99

Alan,

I understand that you have volunteered for my campaign. I am grateful to have you on my team.

Your state is very important to winning back the White House. I am working hard to build a strong grassroots organization to carry MI.

I hope you will continue working hard. Together I am confident we will win.

Sincerely,

George W Bush

Lord Byron

ENGLISH POET (1788–1824)

One of the most controversial of the Romantic poets, George Gordon Byron was born into an aristocratic family living in reduced circumstances. Inheriting the family title and estate at age 10, he published his first book of poetry before the age of 20. With the publication of *Childe Harold's Pilgrimage* in 1812, he recorded, "I woke up and found myself famous." More fame followed with the publication of works including *Don Juan* (1819), and notoriety with a series of passionate love affairs. Byron left England in 1816 for Italy and died eight years later of fever while supporting Greek independence fighters in Missolonghi.

Personality overview

There is a delicacy about Byron's writing that depicts a sensitive soul, but one who existed in isolation. No matter how many people he was involved with, it is likely that Byron always felt alone. There is a strong movement to the right, toward other people, but the wide spatial arrangement is at odds with this slant, creating, or perhaps simply reflecting, the conflict he felt. The personal pronoun, *I*, transmits an attitude of pride, even arrogance, as it stands alone with a straight downstroke that denies dependence.

Relationships

The light pressure and airy layout is another expression of Byron's sensitive, romantic nature. During his lifetime, he suffered many losses, so the gaps between words and between letters could be construed as his defense against getting too close to people and being hurt again. The open lower zone characterizes unresolved issues with the past, and the open curve to the left shows his yearning for love and affection on a very deep level. Although he may have given himself over to the sexual excesses of the often long, lower loops, his needs were left unfulfilled, as the loops never return to the baseline.

Intellectual forces

The writing is well arranged, with simplified forms and no superfluous strokes. Byron was keenly perceptive and astute, and the breaks between letters leave room for intuitive thoughts to burst through into his consciousness. The tall upper zone attests to a focus on philosophical, theoretical thinking in one who could expend much of his energy on the mental plane.

Physical drives

Although there are some fairly long lower loops, and the writing is lively, Byron's energy was probably more on a mental than a physical level. Since this sample was written in the year before his death, his health may have been in a decline. Alternatively the writing's fragile appearance could be due more to his sensitive nature.

Motivating forces

There is a refinement about the script that indicates a love for the aesthetic and luxurious. Byron's surroundings would have had to be congenial and balanced, and he would not have appreciated anything gaudy or tasteless. This is someone for whom beauty and harmony in their purest forms were a major motivating force.

Between the lines

When space between words is so large that it forms a pattern, drawing the eye as it continues down the page, it is called a river. There is literally a river of space. In some cases rivers are the result of visual problems in the writer, in others they indicate some kind of developmental delays. In cases such as Byron's the writer is probably suffering from an inner split—the rivers reveal his or her emotional isolation, their inability to connect with other people.

If you do me the honour of an answer—may
I request a speedy one: because it is possible
(though not yet decided) that Circumstances may
conduct me once more to Greece;—my present
address is Genoa ----
---- I beg you to believe me with
a lively recollection of our brief acquaintance—and
the hope of one day renewing it—your ever obliged
and most humble Servt.
Noel Byron.
Genoa May 29th 1823.

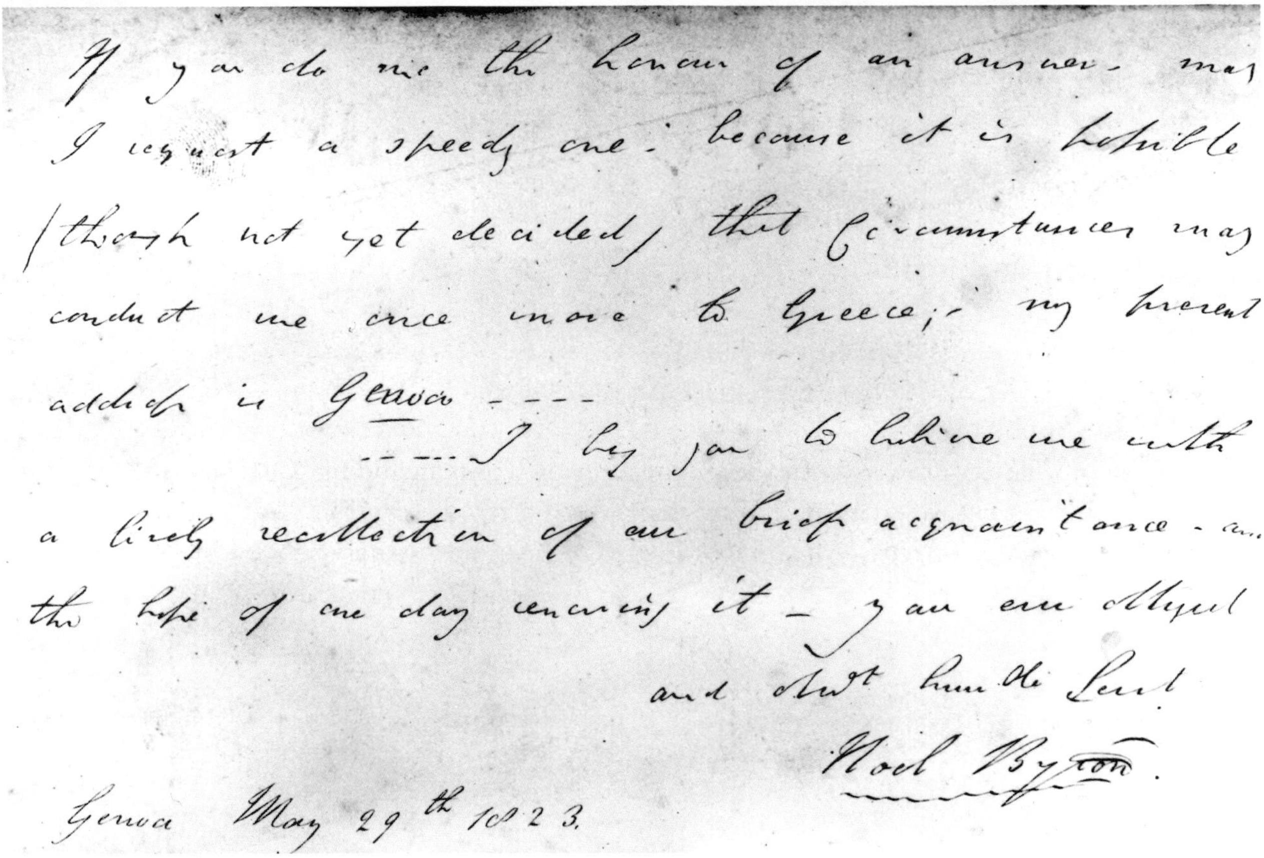

A letter written by Lord Byron

... If you do me the honour of an answer, may I request a speedy one: because it is possible (though not yet decided) that circumstances may conduct me once more to Greece; my present address is Genoa ...

... I beg you to ... me with a lively recollection of our brief acquaintance and the hope of one day ... it—your ever obliged and most humble Servt.

Noel Byron

Genoa, May 29th 1823

Andrew Carnegie

Industrialist, Philanthropist (1835–1919)

Andrew Carnegie was born into a working class family in Scotland and after the family emigrated to the United States in 1848, went to work in a textile mill as a bobbin boy. Here his excellent penmanship soon earned him a promotion to a clerical position and later to a post at the Pennsylvania Railroad. During this time he undertook a number of shrewd investments, and went on to lead the expansion of the American steel industry, eventually becoming known as the richest man in the world. One of the most respected philanthropists of the time, he died August 11, 1919.

Personality overview

A strong characteristic of Carnegie's handwriting is its high degree of regularity, indicating the development of self-discipline. He maintained consistent size in the height and width of the middle zone, which takes concentration and an ability to regulate the movement. A very strong right slant in many upstrokes points to a person of swift emotional responses, but the regularity of movement indicates the control needed for him to think twice before acting.

Relationships

The upper zone is disproportionately tall in relation to the middle zone, revealing a strong sense of responsibility within a rather authoritarian personality. In other words, Carnegie was better at giving orders than taking them. The combination of strong angles and deep garlands show someone who could be firm but caring. The angles lend strength to the garlands, but the garlands soften the angles.

Intellectual forces

Carnegie was willing to explore a variety of new concepts and ideas and the upper-zone emphasis shows he put energy into philosophical thought. The move-ment reaches upward as if seeking answers, and is often seen in the handwriting of very religious people. The smooth breaks within words suggest that he was open to his intuition and might have been willing, occasionally, to go with his instincts. Yet the sharpness of the strokes make the writing seem chiseled, or in relief, a feature of a judgmental person who sees things in black or white.

Physical drives

The pressure appears to be fairly light, suggesting that Carnegie's willpower might have been stronger than his stamina. He could get things done by directing others, as seen in the long *t*-bars, lack of margins, and the inexor-able rightward movement of the sample.

Motivating forces

Carnegie was motivated by pride in his accomplish-ments, as evidenced by the large capitals and tall upper-zone letters. His signature is clear and similar to the body of writing. This shows a direct, candid character whose self-confidence and assertiveness brought him success. The pleasing arrangement of space indicates the ability to keep a clear perspective in order to make practical judgments and decisions.

Between the lines

Regularity in handwriting is part of the rhythm of movement. A highly regular script, such as Carnegie's, is one where all the middle zone letters are the same height and all the downstrokes return, metronomelike, to the baseline. Such regularity takes self-discipline and concentration. At the other end of the spectrum is a highly irregular script, where the middle zone fluctuates widely and many letters fall short of reaching the baseline.

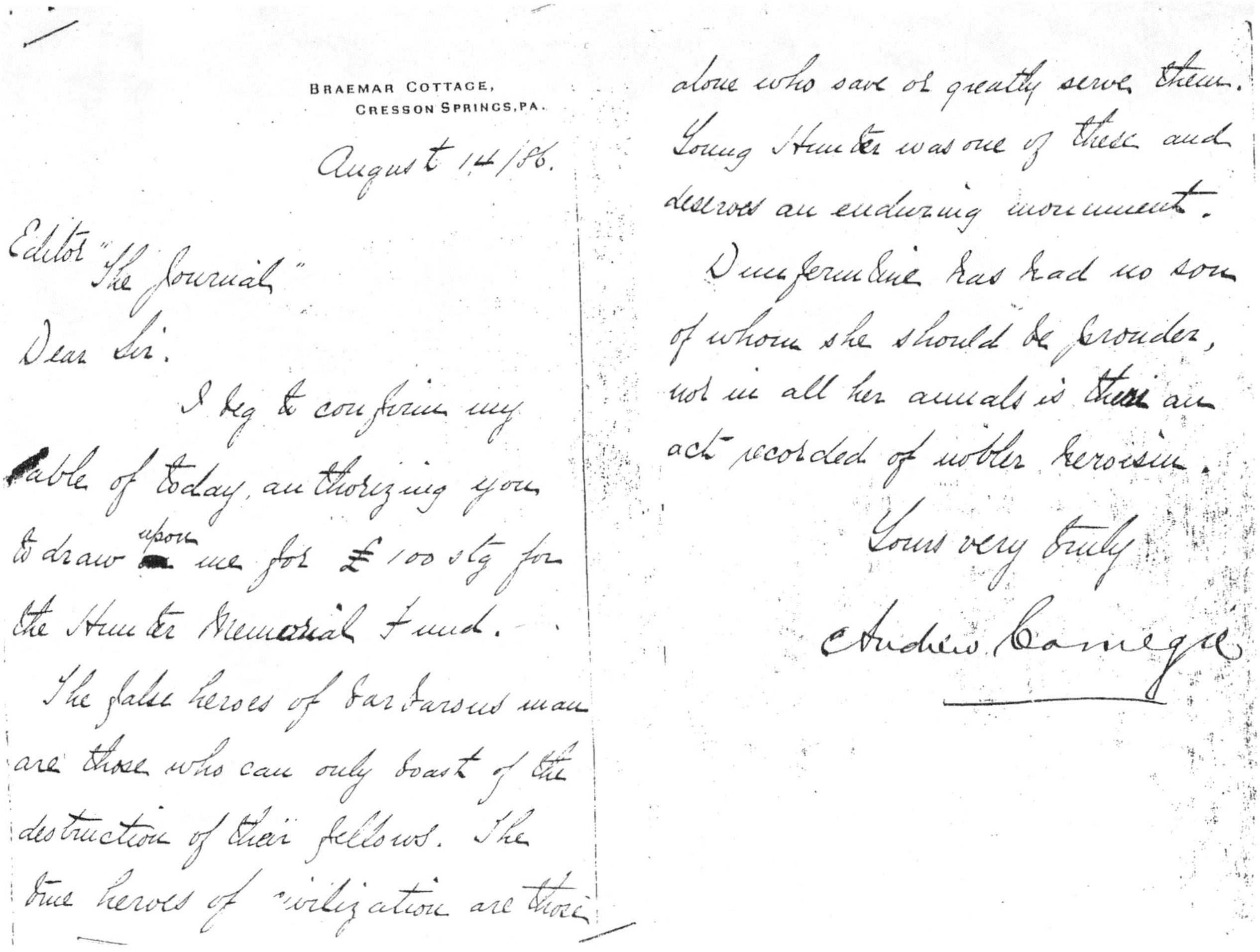

BRAEMAR COTTAGE,
CRESSON SPRINGS, PA.

August 14/86.

Editor "The Journal"

Dear Sir,

I beg to confirm my cable of today, authorizing you to draw upon me for £ 100 stg for the Hunter Memorial Fund.

The false heroes of barbarous man are those who can only boast of the destruction of their fellows. The true heroes of civilization are those alone who save or greatly serve them. Young Hunter was one of these and deserves an enduring monument.

Dunfermline has had no son of whom she should be prouder, nor in all her annals is there an act recorded of nobler heroism.

Yours very truly,

Andrew Carnegie

A letter Carnegie wrote to the editor of *The Journal*, August 14 1886

August 14/86
Editor "The Journal"

Dear Sir,
I beg to confirm my cable of today, authorizing you to draw upon me for £ 100 stg for the Hunter Memorial Fund.
The false heroes of barbarous man are those who can only boast of the destruction of their fellows. The true heroes of civilization are those alone who can save or greatly serve them. Young Hunter was one of these and deserves an enduring monument.
... has had no son of whom she should be prouder, nor in all her annals is there an act recorded of nobler heroism.
Yours very truly,

Andrew Carnegie

Fidel Castro

CUBAN REVOLUTIONARY AND LEADER (1926–   )

Fidel Castro was born on the family sugar plantation in Cuba and began his a career as a lawyer, working to help the poor. Having been heavily involved in politics since university, Castro led a failed revolt against General Batista's government in 1953, spending two years in prison as a result. After subsequent failed attempts, Castro finally recruited enough troops to overthrow Batista in 1959. His government was initially recognized by the United States, but the Bay of Pigs invasion, which was supported by the American CIA, and the Cuban Missile Crisis resulted in ongoing hostilities between the two nations.

Personality overview

This sample of Castro's handwriting was written when he was only 14 years old, and provides a fascinating glimpse into the mind of a boy who grew up to govern his country for more than 40 years. Although his first language is Spanish, he wrote in rather good English. The writing is strongly copybook style, but what is surprising is how well he adhered to this school model, and also how mature for his age the script appears.

Relationships

The writing is very closely spaced and highly connected, revealing a boy whose relationships were very important to him. He needed support and interaction from other people, and probably enjoyed getting feedback. He stayed within conventional boundaries but at the same time could be argumentative, as seen in the tall extensions on the *p*'s, and some long *t*-bars. One can just picture this boy vigorously defending his point of view: he preferred leading to following, even then.

Intellectual forces

Despite the compact spatial arrangement, the overall organization is quite good, especially for a young boy.

The tall upper zone with moderate width loops signifies a person who freely explored the realm of the intellect, keeping an open mind. The height of the loops show that the young Castro was reaching upward, searching for new philosophies to investigate, while the loop-width shows imagination.

Physical drives

A healthy balance exists between the zones, and the writing is executed with energy and vigor. Castro evidently knew from a young age what he wanted to do, and he had the assurance, determination, and persistence to go ahead and do it.

Motivating forces

There is forcefulness in the rightward movement and regularity of the writing. Castro was self-confident as a youth, and already believed in his own power and ability. Interestingly, he had trouble capitalizing the word "American" which may indicate a basic lack of regard for what the word represents. Like many Hispanic signatures, his is written with a great deal of elaboration, yet is still fairly legible. It tells us that he wanted to make his mark, and he wanted the world to know who he was.

*I don't know ve
but I know ve.
Spanish and*

Between the lines

The best known, most popular method of handwriting analysis is loosely based on the French, or empirical, method and is called trait-stroke. Using this method, each stroke in handwriting is assigned a specific personality-trait name. So, for example, there are resentment strokes, self-castigation strokes, yieldingness strokes, and so on. The resulting list of personality traits is fashioned into a picture of the writer's personality.

An extract from a letter written by Castro to Franklin D. Roosevelt

The letter is dated 6 November 1940.

... President of the United States.

If you like, give me a ten dollars bill green american, in the letter, because never, I have not seen a ten dollars bill green american and I would like to have one of them. My address is:

Sr. Fidel Castro, Colegio de Dolores, Santiago de Cuba, Oriente, Cuba.

I don't know very English but I know very much Spanish and I suppose you don't know very Spanish but you know very English because you are American but I am not American.

(Thank you very much.) Good by. Your friend,

Fidel Castro

If you want iron to make your ships I will show to you the biggest (minas) of iron of the land. They are in Mayari. Oriente Cuba.

Catherine the Great

EMPRESS OF RUSSIA (1729–1796)

Born Sophie Friederike Augusta, Catherine married Grand Duke Peter, heir to the Russian throne, when she was 15. The marriage was a disaster and in 1762, with the backing of the Imperial Guard, she caused her unpopular husband to abdicate and became empress of Russia. Peter was assassinated eight days later. Under Catherine's rule, Russia underwent cultural and political reform, and was victorious in two wars against the Ottoman Empire. Catherine, also famed for her many lovers and extravagances, ruled until her death aged 67.

Personality overview

The sample was written while Catherine was very young, possibly when she was still in school. The picture of space is extremely crowded and overly regular, while the style is ornate and embellished. In addition, a great deal of space is taken up by the extra-large capital letters, this being a sign of egocentricity. The letter form is one of slow arcades, which suggest premeditation before acting, and mendacity. The word space is also extremely narrow, but with broad letters, reflecting someone who was both controlling and self-willed.

Relationships

In addition to the crowded spatial arrangement, the slant leans only slightly to the right, which echoes a conflict—the spacing suggests the need for close personal contact, but the slant is not strong enough to indicate much interest in reaching out to others. Also, the word endings are either blunt or curl back to the left, and there are snail-like, rolled-in strokes, which appear to be an exaggeration of the copybook model. These are signs of selfishness and immaturity.

Intellectual forces

The elaboration in the upper zone, with tall letters of reasonable width, are made by someone who had strong intellectual leanings. In this sample Catherine, who was later known to correspond with many of the great thinkers of her day, showed the beginnings of an abiding interest in learning. Considering the strong level of connectedness, any new idea would have had to be based on a firm foundation of logic before she would accept it.

Physical drives

Forceful and energetic, Catherine felt compelled to be where the action was. There is an inexorability about the way the writing moves across the page. She would have had the fortitude to mow down any enemy foolish enough to stand in her way.

Motivating forces

The writing is so slow and careful that it appears etched, rather than naturally done. This suggests sheer willpower would ensure she got what she wanted. By insisting she was right, Catherine left no safe ground for compromise.

Between the lines

Handwriting reveals a tremendous amount of information about how the writer thinks, their emotional state and manifest behavior. However, it would be foolish to claim that it can reveal everything about a person. What we can see is the potential for certain behavior. For example, Catherine's writing has the potential for dishonest behavior, but her writing cannot tell us whether she actually acted on that.

Part of a letter written by Catherine the Great to Tzarina Elisabeth Petrowna

A fault which I have committed for which I very humbly beg pardon from Your Imperial Majesty allows me the happiness to assure you of our successful journey and of the perfect health which his Imperial Majesty the Grand Duke and myself have enjoyed up to now.
This fault concerns a letter from my aunt, who is married to the Prince (of Gobta?), which she is pressing me to deliver as a record of her thanks.

Charlie Chaplin

ENGLISH-BORN ACTOR (1889–1977)

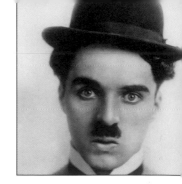

The son of music-hall performers from London, Charlie Chaplin moved to the United States in 1910 as part of a music-hall troupe. Entering the fledgling movie business four years later, Chaplin found fame with his portrayal of such sympathetic characters as "the tramp." He received a special Oscar at the first Academy Awards ceremony in 1929, since when his profound influence on filmmaking has become increasingly apparent. Chaplin married four times and saw more than one scandal along the way. After a long and distinguished career, he made his final film in 1966 and was knighted in 1975.

Personality overview

The emphasis in Chaplin's handwriting is the forceful movement to the right. The many angular formations generally indicate a high degree of tension in the personality. However, since the sample was written in 1967, when he was at an advanced age, health problems may have affected his muscular coordination. Assuming reasonably good health, the angles, heavy pressured *t*-bars, and contraction in the writing point to a hard-driving, dynamic character who would not give up until he had accomplished what he set out to do.

Relationships

Chaplin's right-slanted writing reveals an emotional nature. The spaces between words are quite variable, sometimes quite close and at other times wide, an indication of social variability. This means he might have needed closeness and intimacy one moment, then would suddenly demand his own space. Another aspect of the high degree of angles in the sample is that Chaplin could be demanding. An emotionally responsive person, he also, the angles show, made an effort to contain his impulses. In high-stress situations, however, his self-control might have crumbled.

Intellectual forces

There is a lot of activity in the upper zone, where the *t*-bars are heavy and long and the *i*-dots are formed like little tents and dashes. This indicates that Chaplin not only had many exciting ideas, but also knew how to get them put into practice by directing others to do his bidding.

Physical drives

The angles and heavy horizontal pressure, along with the emphasis on movement, are all hallmarks of dynamic energy. Chaplin had the stamina to get through a long day of work and still keep on going. The lower-zone width is mixed. Excitement and action were high priorities for him, and the straight initial strokes on many words provide a springboard into activity.

Motivating forces

Chaplin's emphatic left-to-right movement in the high, upward pointed *t*-crosses attest to his need to achieve. We could interpret this as characteristic of a person who aims high. The capital letters are in good proportion to the middle-zone height, indicating that his personal accomplishments provided a sense of pride, but he also stayed balanced in his need for the approval of others.

Between the lines

The letter *t* is comprised of several elements, each of which provides important information when looked at as part of the whole writing. The height of the stem shows how tall the writer feels, while the placement of the crossbar indicates how practical his or her goals are. The length of the crossbar, as with Chaplin's distinctive *t*'s, signifies the writer's enthusiasm in pursuing goals, and the pressure on the bar shows how much energy he or she expends in meeting those goals.

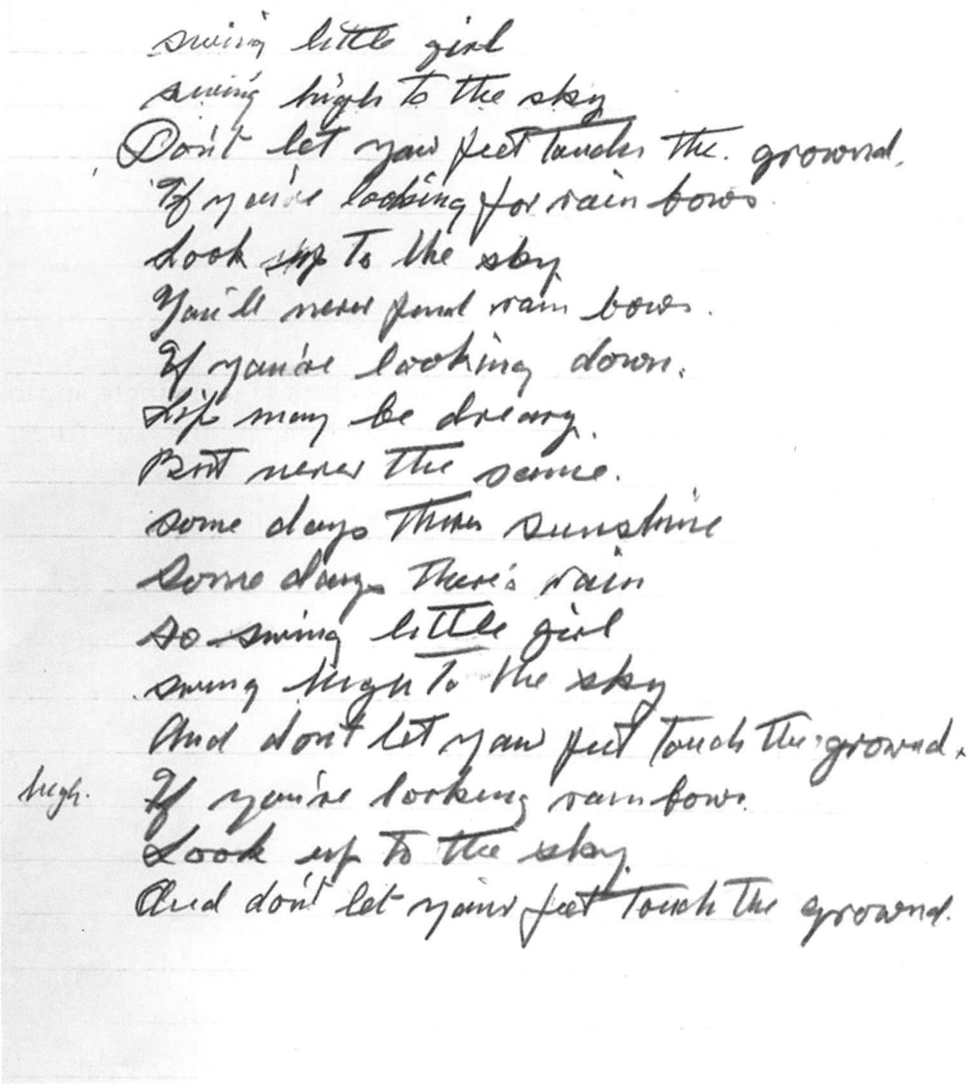

Swing little girl
Swing high to the sky
Don't let your feet touch the ground
If you're looking for rainbows
Look up to the sky
You'll never find rainbows
If you're looking down
Life may be dreary
But never the same
Some days there's sunshine
Some days there's rain
So swing little girl
Swing high to the sky
And don't let your feet touch the ground
If you're looking rainbows
Look up to the sky
And don't let your feet touch the ground.

Song for the musical "Soundtrack to the Circus"

Swing little girl
Swing high to the sky
Don't let your feet touch the ground
If you're looking for rainbows
Look up to the sky
You'll never find rainbows
If you're looking down
Life may be dreary
But never the same

Some days there's sunshine
Some days there's rain
So swing little girl
Swing high to the sky
And don't let your feet touch the ground
If you're looking (for) rainbows
Look up to the sky
And don't let your feet touch the ground

Winston Churchill

BRITISH STATESMAN (1874–1965)

Winston Churchill was born in Oxfordshire, England, to a son of the seventh Duke of Marlborough and Jennie Jerome, an American heiress. Soldier, writer, artist, and politician, Churchill first entered Parliament in 1901 after distinguished service in the Boer War. As prime minister, nearly 40 years later, he led Britain through the devastation of World War II, fighting beside the United States and the Soviet Union to eventual victory against Hitler's Germany. He lost the election after the war, but returned to power in 1951. Churchill died in London on January 24, 1965.

Personality overview

The handwriting is modest and unadorned, well arranged and balanced, symbolizing a personality possessing the same characteristics. Churchill knew his own worth, and did not feel the need to announce it from the rooftops. His capital letters are just the right height—twice the height of the middle zone—and simple. There are no elaborations or pretensions, which implies that he presented himself in a forthright manner and was willing to be accountable for his actions.

Relationships

The romantic side to Churchill's personality is evidenced by the small garland forms and the warm color of the writing. However, wide spaces between the words suggest that he would not crowd those close to him and that he needed a large amount of personal space in which to operate. A moderate right slant indicates that he expressed his emotions but was not bowled over by them.

Intellectual forces

Using both logical and intuitive thought processes, Churchill trusted his instincts but backed up his first reactions with the facts. Although there are few breaks within words, those that do appear are smooth, which signifies one who is comfortable leaving an opening for intuitive thoughts to flow in. The letters connect in fairly long sequences, symbolic of how he strung his thoughts together in a logical sequence, building one idea upon another.

Physical drives

At the time of writing, Churchill was clearly energetic and had plenty of stamina. He channeled his energy where it was needed at the time, with no particular emphasis on one area over another. The bowed *t*-bars are signs of a person who might bend under pressure, but never break. There is a very nice rhythm in this sample, and as a younger man he was probably quite graceful and light on his feet.

Motivating forces

Churchill was motivated by love and a desire to serve others. We see this in the smooth garland forms and in the simplicity of the writing. The attention to detail, such as the carefully dotted *i*'s, and the firm rightward movement indicate one who stuck loyally to his promises and commitments.

Between the lines

The way a page is organized tells a great deal about a writer's approach to life. A well-organized handwriting sample, such as Churchill's, is symbolic of one who is able to set priorities and pursue his or her objectives effectively. On the other hand, a messy sample, with loops hanging down and interfering with the line below, where the margins wander all over the place and the baseline meanders across the page, is made by a writer who has a disorderly mind.

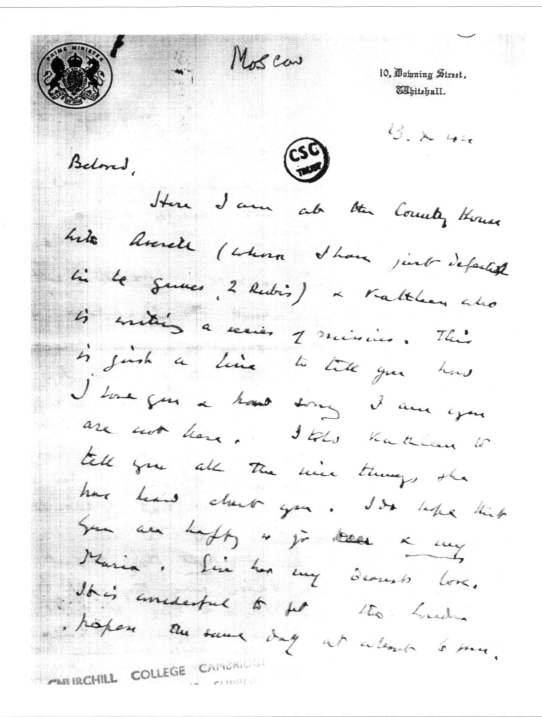

Extract from a letter written by Winston Churchill

Moscow
13.X 44

   Beloved,
   Here I am at the Country House with ... (whom I have just defeated him in 4 games, 2 ...) & Kathleen who is writing a series of missives. This is just a line to tell you how I love you & how sorry I am you are not here. I told Kathleen to tell you all the nice things she has heard about you. I do hope that you are happy ... & my Maria. Give her my dearest love. It is wonderful to get the London papers the same day at about 6 pm ...

Bill Clinton

42ND U.S. PRESIDENT (1946–   )

William Jefferson Clinton was inspired to enter politics when, as a delegate to Boy's Nation, he met John F. Kennedy. Born in Arkansas, he served several terms as Governor there before twice being elected president of the United States in 1993 and 1997. His focus during his presidency was to boost the standard of living for low- and middle-income families, reduce the deficit, create a trade agreement with Mexico, and to control the purchase of guns. Bill Clinton probably survived more scandals than any other American leader over the course of his administration.

Personality overview

Bill Clinton's handwriting is a mixture of curves and angles: the angles give strength to the curves and the curves soften the angles. Thus, he is an emotional person who feels things deeply, someone who will go to some lengths to create a consensus. Yet, when he strongly believes in something he has the capacity to stand firm in his viewpoint. The overall picture of space is compact, indicating a strong need for social contact and genuine caring for the welfare of others.

Relationships

Rounded writing is generally seen as a more feminine quality. When it appears in a man's script it is interpreted as emotional softness, an indicator of one whose heart is easily touched. It can be seen that Clinton both laughs and cries easily and is not ashamed to show his feelings. Another aspect of the round forms exemplified by this handwriting sample is a need for physical contact. He is someone who touches others frequently, and enjoys hugging and holding them close. Triangles in the lower zone hint at subconscious aggression toward women, but since the angles are not sharp in this case, this aggression is expressed indirectly.

Intellectual forces

The upper zone is not well developed, which certainly does not point to a lack of intellect in this case. Instead it shows that Clinton has a greater interest in concrete, day-to-day activities and the application of ideas, rather than in spending a lot of time philosophizing.

Physical drives

The middle and lower zones are accentuated at the expense of the upper zone, revealing an active person who feels compelled to get involved in whatever is going on around him. The crowded nature of the spatial arrangement tells us that Clinton wants to cram as much as possible into each day. The lower zone returns to the baseline, so he usually completes what he starts.

Motivating forces

Clinton's predominantly rounded writing style suggests that his most important motivation is the need to help and serve others. Failing in this would leave him feeling useless and miserable. He needs to know that he has made a difference. The capital *B* in his signature, which is larger than his surname initial, demonstrates a desire for others to think of him as "Bill," more than "Mr. Clinton."

Between the lines

In any handwriting sample the upper-zone height relates to several areas, including the writer's view of authority. An extremely tall upper zone is found in someone who has had a very strict upbringing, often in a highly religious family. This type of person reveres, or perhaps fears, authority figures and is rule-oriented. A short upper zone, as exemplified by Clinton's writing, reveals a writer who sees him- or herself as the only authority to whom he or she should answer.

[Handwritten letter reproduced below in print]

A letter written by Bill Clinton asking for a donation to party funds

Dear Supporter,
I'll never forget your help in 1992, when so many had written us off.
We won because of our commitment to change and because we got our message out.

As you can see from the attached report card on our first 21 months, we've made a good start. We've got a lot left to do, but America is in better shape than it was two years ago: government is working more for ordinary citizens; there are more jobs and lower deficits; and America is leading a worldwide effort to greater security, trade, and democracy.

As you can also see from the attached report, the Congressional Republicans have a very different idea about our future. They've opposed most of the progress we've made. They killed important bills. Their "Contract" is a promise to take us back to trickle down Reaganomics, to exploding deficits, medical cuts, jobs going overseas.

I need your help. In May House and Senate races new Democrats are threatened by old Republicans filling the airwaves with false charges and false choices. We can only beat back their assault with your help. Please send us a check now—anything you can afford. $50 now is worth more than $100 in a week. And share this report with your friends and neighbors. Copy it. Fax it. Help in your local campaigns. The people won't be misled if they get the facts! Sincerely, Bill Clinton

Hillary Clinton

AMERICAN FIRST LADY, SENATOR (1947–   )

Hillary Rodham Clinton became involved in politics at a young age, and headed a chapter of the Young Republicans while attending Wellesley College in the 1960s. She later switched her allegiance to the Democratic Party and went on to study law at Yale, where she became active as a champion for children's rights. She was twice named one of the nation's top 100 most influential lawyers. As First Lady, Hillary Clinton often found herself the subject of controversy and, like Eleanor Roosevelt, was loved and hated with equal fervor. In 2000 she became the first wife of a president to be elected to the Senate.

Personality overview

Hillary Clinton's handwriting is simplified and rhythmic, denoting a manner that is both forthright and candid, although not without charm. The generally linear style is softened with enough curves to allow for sensitivity in dealing with others. All nonessential strokes have been cut away, leaving only what is necessary for understanding and direct communication. This no-frills type of writing means that you can count on her to say what she means and to mean what she says. She does not have the patience for anything less.

Relationships

Highly independent, Clinton does not like feeling hemmed in. She insists on making her own choices and decisions, and must be at least an equal partner in any relationship. The connective form she uses is a mixture of garlands and threads, so she can be diplomatic when she needs to be. However, the short endings on many words, plus abrupt breaks within words, indicate that there are times when diplomacy is not in her vocabulary.

Intellectual forces

A simplified writing style is a major characteristic of someone interested in the theoretical, abstract world of ideas, someone who is open to alternative concepts. The quick *th* connection reflects resourcefulness in one who is good at coming up with new ways of doing things. The lower zone is developed well enough to indicate that she also has the capacity to put those concepts to work in practical ways.

Physical drives

The writing is lively and brisk in its movement, showing stamina and endurance. The zonal balance and blunt downstrokes in the lower zone reflect someone who has learned to use her energy wisely. Hillary Clinton crosses her *t*'s mid-stem and the crosses are longer than the copybook model prescribes. This denotes a person who is practical in the goals she sets, and that her energy is adequate for what she wants to accomplish.

Motivating forces

Hillary Clinton's handwriting has an open, airy appearance, which is often seen in highly progressive individuals. She is driven to make improvements in her environment and in the world more generally. In fact, with her original letter forms, it would be impossible for her not to innovate and continually seek out ways in which to do things better.

Between the lines

Rhythm in handwriting is a very difficult concept to understand, but it is one of the most important characteristics to learn to identify. Many different types of rhythm exist along a wide spectrum, with typewriterlike regularity at one end, and a stormy, uneven style at the other. Hillary's rhythm is midway between the two—elastic with a good balance between contraction and release. Rhythm reveals personality integration, or how all the various aspects of the writer's personality fit together.

Thanks for your encouragement and support. With your help and support, we'll have a great victory on November 3rd. Best wishes— Hillary

Note written by Hillary Clinton to a supporter

Thanks for your encouragement and support. With your help and support, we'll have a great victory on November 3rd .
Best wishes—
Hillary

Kurt Cobain

AMERICAN MUSICIAN (1967–1994)

When Kurt Cobain killed himself on April 5, 1994, his cult status and that of his "grunge" rock band, Nirvana, skyrocketed. Cobain was a troubled teenager, dropping out of school and taking various jobs before forming the band in 1986. Nirvana put out their first album in 1989, followed two years later by the phenomenally successful *Nevermind*. Throughout much of the band's time in the charts, Cobain's relationship with another pop icon, Courtney Love, attracted as much media attention his music. Cobain, depressed and addicted to heroin, shot himself shortly after checking out of a rehabilitation clinic.

Personality overview

The handwriting in Kurt Cobain's suicide letter is painful to view, and reveals a desperately unhappy person, unable to reconcile himself to success. When troubled by adversity he was often inclined to bail out without putting up much of a fight. The crowded spacing of the writing, poor rhythm, and wavy baseline imply that he could see only the problems facing him at the time, while overlooking any potential solutions. In the printed form is a strong spirit of independence, a desire to take charge of his own destiny and make his own decisions. This Cobain ultimately did, of course, in taking his own life.

Relationships

Cobain's strong need and desire to be close to other people, as seen in the cramped picture of space, is at odds with the sterile printed forms. The variability in size and slant of the middle zone also reveal a highly sensitive person, one who was easily torn by the conflicts that seemed to continuously assail him. The printed letter *a* indicates inner suffering in someone who perceived himself as having been abused in some way, probably early in life.

Intellectual forces

At the time of writing, Cobain was unable to see the forest for the trees. His perspective on life was skewed—whatever was troubling him was crowding in to such a degree that he could not see anything else. As a result, common sense was not something he could rely on.

Physical drives

Again, the crowded spacing and undulating baseline show that Cobain often felt overwhelmed by the degree of turmoil he endured, and he struggled against a continual sense of self-doubt. Regulating his emotional impulses, even in relatively uneventful times, could be too much of a challenge. The variable style also indicates a low degree of self-control. He did whatever felt good at the moment, even when he knew it was bad for him. Anything to dull the emotional pain.

Motivating forces

This handwriting reflects inner chaos, yet Kurt Cobain craved harmony. He needed the time, space, and autonomy to do what energized him, yet, while he might have been able to get those needs met on the outside, he was not able to give that space to himself.

Between the lines

Some graphologists have observed that the printed *a* with its covering stroke over the top of the letter (as seen in Kurt Cobain's handwriting), is often made by those people who have suffered abuse in childhood. As the middle zone is the area of communication, the covering stroke hides information. However, this form is also seen in the writing of highly creative people. As always in handwriting analysis, interpretation depends upon context.

... I'm too sensi ...
I once had as a child. On our last 3 tours I've had a much better appreciation
... all the people I've known personally and as fans of our music, but I still can't set out
... frustration, the guilt and empathy I have for everyone. There's good in all of us and I ...
... I simply love people too much. So much that it makes me feel too fucking sad. The sad ...
... ive, sensitive, unappreciative, pisces, Jesus man! why don't you just enjoy it? I don't k...
have a goddess of a wife who sweats ambition and empathy ... and a daughter who rem...
... too much of what I used to be. full of love and joy, passing every person she meets
cause everyone is good and will do her no harm. And that terrifies me to the point to where I ca...
...ly function. I can't stand the thought of Frances becoming the miserable self destructive,
...self rocker that I've become. I have it good. very Good. and I'm grateful, but si...
...s age of seven I've become hateful towards all humans in general.. Only because it seems s...
...sy for people to get along and have empathy. Empathy! Only because I love and feel s...
... people too much I guess. Thank you all from the pit of my burning nauseo...
...stomach for your letters and concern during the past years. I'm too much of an erratic, moody...
...don't have the passion anymore and so remember, its better to burn out than to...
fade away . peace, love, Empathy.

Frances and Courtney, I'll be at our altar.
please keep going Courtney(s)

CAPT Kurt Khaus.

for Frances
-for her life which will be so much happier
without me..   I lOVE YOU, I LOVE YOU

Part of Kurt Cobain's suicide note, addressed to Courtney Love and his daughter

   ... I once had as a child. On our last 3 tours I've had a much better appreciation ... all the people I've known personally and as fans of our music, but I still can't ... on ... frustration, the guilt and empathy I have for everyone. There's good in all of us and I ... I simply love people too much. So much that it makes me feel too fucking sad. The sad ... sensitive, unappreciative pisces, Jesus man! Why don't you just enjoy it? I don't ... a goddess of a wife who sweats ambition and empathy and a daughter who reminds me too much of what I used to be. full of love and joy, ... every person she meets cause everyone is good and will do her no harm. And that terrifies me to the point to where I ... function. I can't stand the thought of Frances becoming the miserable, self destructive ... that I've become. I have it good. Very Good. And I'm grateful, but since the age of seven I've become hateful towards all humans in general. Only because it seems so easy for people to get along and have empathy. Empathy! Only because I love and feel ... people too much I guess. Thank you all from the pit of my burning nauseous stomach for your letters and concern during the past years. I'm too much of an erratic, moody ... don't have the passion anymore and so remember it's better to burn out than to fade away. peace, love, Empathy. Kurt Cobain
   Frances and Courtney, I'll be at our altar. Please keep going Courtney for Frances for her life which will be so much happier without me. I love you. I LOVE YOU ...

Christopher Columbus

GENOAN NAVIGATOR (1451–1506)

Navigator Christopher Columbus was convinced of the existence of a westward sea route to the Spice Islands of the East Indies and spent 10 years seeking backing for an Atlantic voyage. He prevailed upon the Spanish court of Ferdinand and Isabella and under their flag reached Hispaniola in 1492; three more voyages took him to other Caribbean islands and South America. Despite his renown, the "discoverer" of the Americas died disappointed and disillusioned by his lack of reward from the Spanish crown.

Personality overview

This handwriting sample may have been written at a time of stress, or perhaps illness, as Columbus' basic writing movement mixes a good distribution of pressure and apparent speed with tremor in some strokes and a convex baseline. Add the upward diagonal movement and intermittent bursts of energy, enthusiasm, and initiative can be seen, mixed with doubt and discouragement.

Relationships

The writing shows confidence, with its proportionate capital letters and simplification of form. Columbus' persuasiveness can also be seen in the thready forms, which creep in among the firmer arcades and a few angles. Close word spacing suggests someone who welcomed the company of others, but the changeable slant, size, and baseline are indicators of moodiness, which probably made him difficult to get along with.

Intellectual forces

The strong movement into the upper zone is evidence of Columbus' exploratory interests and curiosity about discovering new worlds, even if only intellectually. Of course, he went well beyond intellectual discovery, and the long forays into the lower zone indicate that he had what it took to turn his dreams into reality.

Physical drives

The pressure appears to fluctuate, but the overall pattern of light and dark strokes is well distributed, indicating a balance between the control and release of emotions. The writing seems to have a nervous energy, a sense of impatience to be on the move. The baseline moves upward then falls down, which is a sign of someone whose enthusiasm waxed and waned.

Motivating forces

Columbus had strong aspirations, seen particularly in the movement into the upper zone and to the right. The wide upper loops are containers for his imagination and openness to new undertakings, and show that he was willing to venture into unfamiliar territory. The buoyant quality of the writing suggests one who was enchanted more by possibilities than by what actually existed.

Between the lines

Natural writing is free-flowing, and is adopted by a spontaneous person who does not spend a lot of time and energy on creating an image. Once the student has learned and becomes comfortable with handwriting, he or she no longer has to think about each stroke and letter as they are written. This is known as graphic maturity, can be seen in Columbus' script, and is required for natural writing.

Extract from a letter from Columbus to the Bank of Saint George, April 2, 1502

The Grand Admiral of the Ocean Sea and viceroy and governor general of the islands and mainland of Asia and the Indies for the king and queen, my lords, and your captain general of the sea and of your council (?)
    .S.
    .S.A.S.
    X M Y
Xpo FERENS

Marie Curie

POLISH-BORN FRENCH SCIENTIST (1867–1934)

Born Marie Sklodowska, Marie Curie is famous for investigating radioactivity and for twice winning the Nobel prize, once (for physics) with Henri Becquerel and her husband, Pierre Curie, in 1903, and then as the sole winner of the prize for chemistry in 1911. Both physical chemists, the Curies worked together to discover two new elements, polonium and radium, and had two daughters before Pierre's sudden death in 1906. Marie Curie continued their work, became the first woman to teach at the Sorbonne in Paris, and went on to develop the use of X-radiography. Curie eventually died of leukemia, the result of exposure to radiation.

Personality overview

Curie's handwriting has a beautifully balanced flow and rhythm—there is neither too much emphasis on contraction nor too much on release. This indicates that she could express her feelings in appropriate ways and at the right time. The slight emphasis on the arcade form in this broad spatial arrangement tells us she was a private, conservative person who respected history and tradition, even while she may have challenged it.

Relationships

There is a good distribution of garland forms among the arcades, which is a sign of receptiveness. The rightward slant blends with a moderately strong degree of connectedness to reveal someone who cared about others, even though she might not have always been able to show it. That she was not very demonstrative is evidenced in the wide word spacing and long end strokes. The end strokes are sometimes used to fill up the ends of lines, signifying a degree of distrust in others.

Intellectual forces

The excellent arrangement of space, with balanced margins and line spacing, is the hallmark of one who knew how to create a reasonable framework within which to operate. The writing has the quick tempo and smooth rhythm of one who could move rapidly from one problem to the next, using her intuition and resourcefulness, as seen in the original, simplified letter forms.

Physical drives

The overall writing rhythm is elastic, and the lower zone is well-formed in length and width, demonstrating an enthusiasm for life, an ability to roll with the punches and bounce back without undue stress. Add the long, well-pressured *t*-crosses, and Curie could handle a long day of work and still be ready for more. The hooks on the beginnings and endings of some words suggest one who could be quite persistent in the pursuit of her goals.

Motivating forces

The need to produce is evident in this vital, animated script. With the large capital letters, especially on her name, Curie was not averse to being acknowledged for her contributions. However, she signs only "*M*," rather than her full name, so it is doubtful whether recognition was the motivating factor behind her efforts. Rather, she was proud of who she was and what that meant.

Between the lines

By comparing a handwriting sample to the copybook model taught in the country where the writer went to school, the writing of someone of any nationality can be analyzed using Gestalt principles. English and Cyrillic are the only languages that use a single letter as the personal pronoun, and some languages do not use zones. However, all writing samples have margins, letter, line, and word spacing, and all have speed, pressure, and other characteristics.

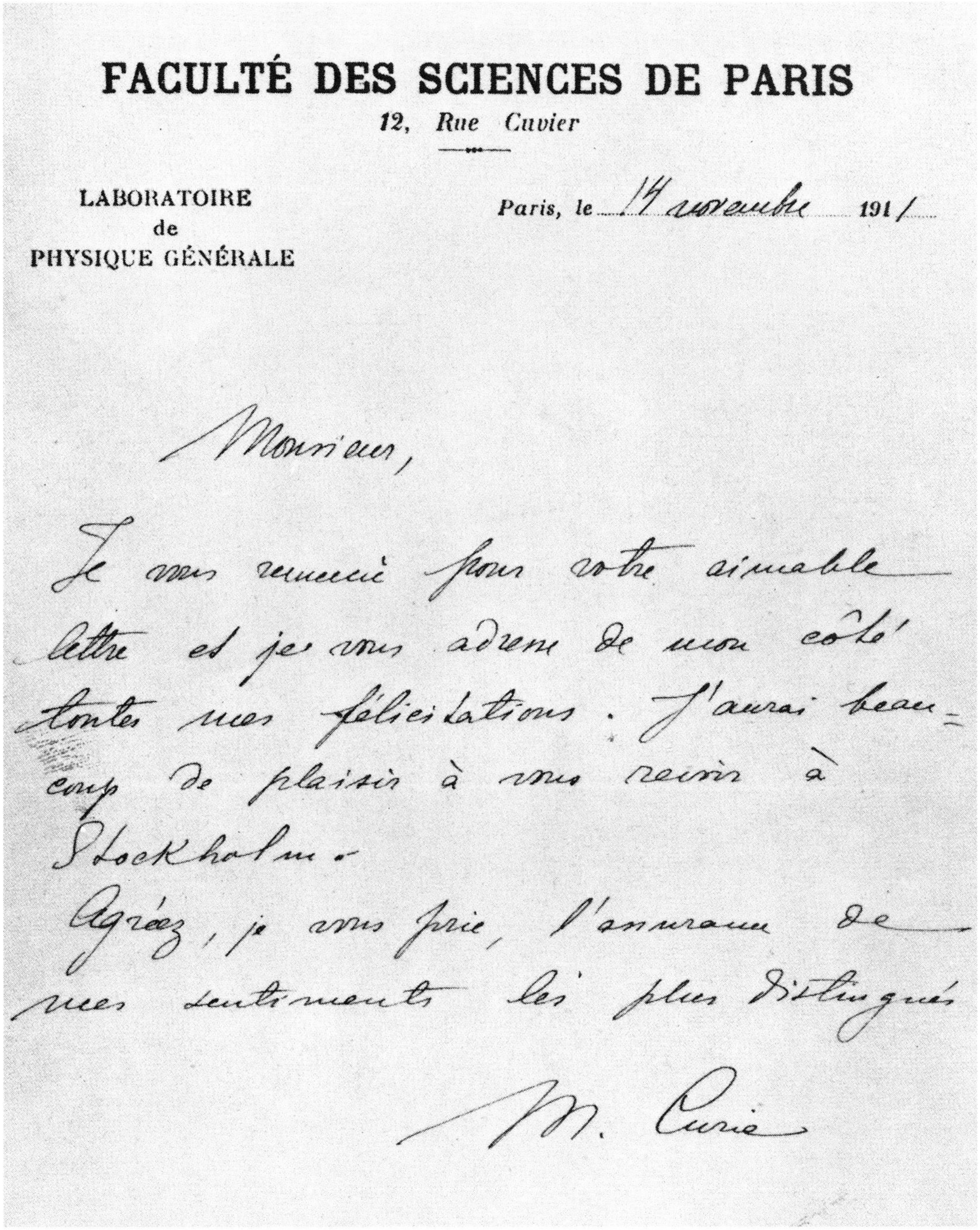

FACULTÉ DES SCIENCES DE PARIS

12, Rue Cuvier

LABORATOIRE
de
PHYSIQUE GÉNÉRALE

Paris, le *14 novembre* 191*1*

Monsieur,

Je vous remercie pour votre aimable lettre et je vous adresse de mon côté toutes mes félicitations. J'aurai beaucoup de plaisir à vous revoir à Stockholm.

Agréez, je vous prie, l'assurance de mes sentiments les plus distingués

M. Curie

A note written by Marie Curie

Paris, 14 November 1911(?)

Mariam,
 I thank you for your nice letter and on my part I would also like to give you my best wishes. It would give me a lot of pleasure to see you again in Stockholm.
 Yours most sincerely,

M. Curie

George Custer

U.S. Soldier (1839–1876)

George Armstrong Custer, born in Ohio, was only 23 when he was appointed brigadier general of volunteers commanding a Michigan cavalry brigade in the Civil War. In the final days of the conflict, his pursuit of Robert E. Lee hastened the eventual surrender of the Confederacy in 1865. Custer's campaigns against Plains Indians in the West made the flamboyant commander of the 7th Cavalry one of the most feted soldiers of the day. On June 25, 1876, Custer and 200 men were surrounded and killed by Dakota (Sioux) and Northern Cheyenne Indians at Little Bighorn.

Personality overview
Custer's bold, expanded handwriting reveals an adventurer. The predominant connective form is angles, with some garlands, too, and the *t*-crosses are often made with the downward pointing stroke of a dominating personality. He clearly had very strong opinions and would brook no interference once he gave a directive. There is a certain impulsiveness in the speedy tempo. The writing takes up a lot of space, and with the large, well-formed capital letters, it is apparent that Custer thought quite well of himself.

Relationships
The writing is right slanted, leaning toward other people, which denotes a sociable person. However, even though he may have had a tender side, Custer was undoubtedly a difficult person to please. The high degree of angles and pointed strokes are made by an authoritarian individual who would expect his rules to be obeyed to the letter. He could, however, motivate others with his drive and energy.

Intellectual forces
Writers with many angles view everything in sharp contrast: yes or no, black or white, right or wrong. There is no gray area. The tall upper zone reveals a man of principle who would not accept less of himself than absolute adherence to the standards he had chosen.

Physical drives
Custer's angular writing is simple, with few extra strokes. From this we can see that he abhorred any waste of time, energy, or resources, and would always take the most direct route. A hard worker, he would pour his energy tirelessly into whatever he had committed to do—as seen in the long, high *t*-crossings—not letting up until the work was done. The sharpness of the writing also reflects a refusal to compromise. When obstacles arose, he would be relentless in mowing them down.

Motivating forces
Custer was driven to take command and was less concerned with the feelings of others than with the results of their efforts. The *t*'s are crossed at the very tops of the stems indicating that Custer set his sights high. Clearly it was not easy to meet the goals he set either for himself or his subordinates. His signature is simple and direct, congruent with the text of the writing sample itself, showing that what you saw was what you got without pretension.

Between the lines
Retracing refers to letters that should have loops, but where the downstroke, instead of leaving a space, covers over the upstroke. In the upper zone, as in Custer's writing (especially on the *t* and *h*), retracing is the sign of a closed mind: no room is left for new ideas. In the lower zone it signifies insecurity and anxiety. In the middle zone, retracing relates to some form of closed-off communication.

A letter written by General Custer to Colonel C. Ross-Smith, November 28 1863

Written in pencil to Smith, General Meade's Chief of Staff, Custer reports of troop entrenchments.

... and a help in their direction. Yesterday P.M. the office in ... of which reported (?) the existence of a strong line of entrenchments. From personal examination I am able to report that the earthworks are of the most formidable ... a strong ... is in front of the active line. In some parts there are two lines of .... The ditch in front of the works is ... but deep, the ... works are revetted along the .... also the ...

I am about to ascertain whether the enemy is in ... in my front or not.

Very Respectfully etc.

G. A. Custer

Brig General

Charles Darwin

ENGLISH NATURALIST (1809–1882)

Charles Darwin studied classics, medicine, and theology, but it was not until he took a position as a naturalist on the HMS *Beagle* in 1831 that he found his true calling. During the voyage Darwin became certain of the gradual evolution of species. After more than 20 years refining his ideas, and by this time battling ill health, he published the controversial *On the Origin of Species by Means of Natural Selection*, in 1859. This was followed by several other volumes. Darwin was not the first naturalist to propose the idea of evolution, but is probably its best known proponent.

Personality overview

Darwin's handwriting has the light, airy quality often associated with the scripts of philosophers and other intellectual types. Light pressure and large intervals between words and lines create islands of space that serve to isolate him on a social level, but simultaneously give him room to think. Darwin was clearly a loner who required a great deal of time and space on his own in which to develop the ideas that proliferated in his cerebral upper zone.

Relationships

Considering the wide spatial arrangement and small middle zone of the writing sample, anyone in a relationship with Darwin would have had to be highly independent and happy to amuse themselves. He could be seen as an absent-minded professor type, with little patience for the niceties of polite conversation. He was probably the type of person who is most comfortable working for long periods of time alone in his study and who often forgets to come down for dinner. It is likely that Darwin was insensitive to the emotional needs of the people around him, not because he did not care, but simply because he was too wrapped up in his own ideas to be aware of them.

Intellectual forces

Again, the wide spaces, coupled with the highly simplified forms, point to intelligence and the ability to simplify matters down to their most basic components. Many of the long *t*-crosses are placed at the very tops of the stems, indicating idealism and high ideas, but because they maintain contact with the stem, Darwin's ideas stayed within the realm of reality. The poor legibility suggests that he was so involved in complicated thoughts and concepts he might assume he had spoken an idea aloud, even when it was just in his head.

Physical drives

Darwin lived life chiefly on an intellectual level. He might have had greater physical energy earlier in life, but at the time of writing (1871) his energy was directed into the mental plane, as evidenced in the upper-zone emphasis (long, high *t*-bars) and the strong simplification of form.

Motivating forces

Forward-thinking, continually striving to improve his ideas and methods and make them more efficient, Darwin's stunted lower zone shows that he had little use for the material world. Instead he was motivated by the possibilities inherent in any situation.

Between the lines

Writing is for the purpose of communicating. Someone, such as Darwin, who does not bother to make his or her writing legible perpetrates a hostile act on the reader, who is frustrated by his or her inability to read the words the writer has put down on paper. Illegibility may be an attempt to hide information, or simply to be evasive. Clear, legible writing, on the other hand, reveals someone who has nothing to hide, but is up front and candid in his or her communications.

The Descent of Man, and Selection in Relation to Sex (1871)

Taken from an autographed manuscript, this shows sheet 7 of a design for the introduction to the above work.

Charles Darwin — Introduction — Descent of Man
is descended from ... other from lower on the scale, so that it was necessary (?) for me to consider the subject. I likewise wished to ascertain how far to ... the effect seen of man. Every reader can judge for himself whether I have succeeded in throwing any little additional light on this ..., though ... important, subject.

James Dean

American Actor (1931–1955)

Following the death of his mother, James Dean was raised on a farm in Indiana by an aunt and uncle. He enrolled in James Whitmore's acting workshop while attending college at UCLA, and later moved to New York. Here he attracted Hollywood attention and made his screen debut in *East of Eden* in 1955. This was followed soon after by *Rebel Without a Cause* (1955) and *Giant* (1956), but Dean was killed in a car crash prior to his third film's release. Even in this short time he had become a symbol of the rebellious, idealistic youth of his day. His early death contributed to this cult status, both at the time and since.

Personality overview

To those who thought of him as a symbol of machismo, Dean's handwriting may come as a surprise. A soft, almost feminine quality suggests a deeply sensitive side. The droopy garland connecting strokes indicate someone who would have gone out of his way to make sure everyone got along as well as possible. Although the garlands tell us he was emotionally based, the upright to slight-left slant of the upper loops reveal that he would not have allowed his emotions to overcome him. Dean's personal pronoun, *I*, starts at the bottom, which reverses the traditional Palmer school model and reflects his conflict about losing his mother so early in life.

Relationships

The lack of strong forward movement in Dean's writing, along with the soft forms and dark-colored strokes, shows an easygoing nature with an ability to get along with most people. Add to that the flexible baseline and we see a congenial, warm individual with a sense of humor.

Intellectual forces

A good sense of organization can be seen in the clear line spacing and well-proportioned letters. Dean obviously had the capacity to plan ahead, equipping himself with whatever he needed in order to meet his objectives. However, the short *t*-crosses suggest he might not have had the confidence to look too far into the future, and he probably set his goals at practical levels.

Physical drives

The generally thick pen strokes (pastosity) reflect a sensuous person who loved the good life and who, without controlling factors, could have been self-indulgent. Periodically the stroke becomes even thicker, flooding the line of writing with ink. It is likely that Dean especially enjoyed the sense of touch, yet the incomplete lower zone shows that it was difficult for him to satisfy his needs for physical contact.

Motivating forces

In the handwriting sample the upper and lower zones are emphasized at the expense of the middle zone, which indicates Dean's avoidance of some issues relating to his day-to-day life. It can be seen that he was throwing his energy into intellectual and physical pursuits, probably to take his mind off whatever it was that was troubling him.

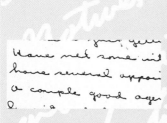

Between the lines

The shape of the strokes connecting one letter to the next reveals social attitudes. The four major types of connecting strokes are garlands, arcades, angles, and thread. Garlands, the main connective form in Dean's writing, are cup-shaped and are made by warm, friendly people. Arcades are also cup-shaped, but the cup is upside down, offering a hiding place. Angles are straight lines, indicating firmness, and thread is an indefinite form made by those who avoid commitment.

Career business is just getting under way. Have met some interesting people and have several appointments next week. A couple good agents are intensely interested. (note intensely) This crazy world seems to be a continuous chase around the table. Nature has patterned it so that I must run in the opposite direction to complete the game. Boy! I'm running? It's a tiring game but I'm younger. Horrible!!

Give my love to your charming mother, Mrs? Riggs, Mrs Buckhart and take a little yourself.

Buenos Suerte

Siempre James Dean

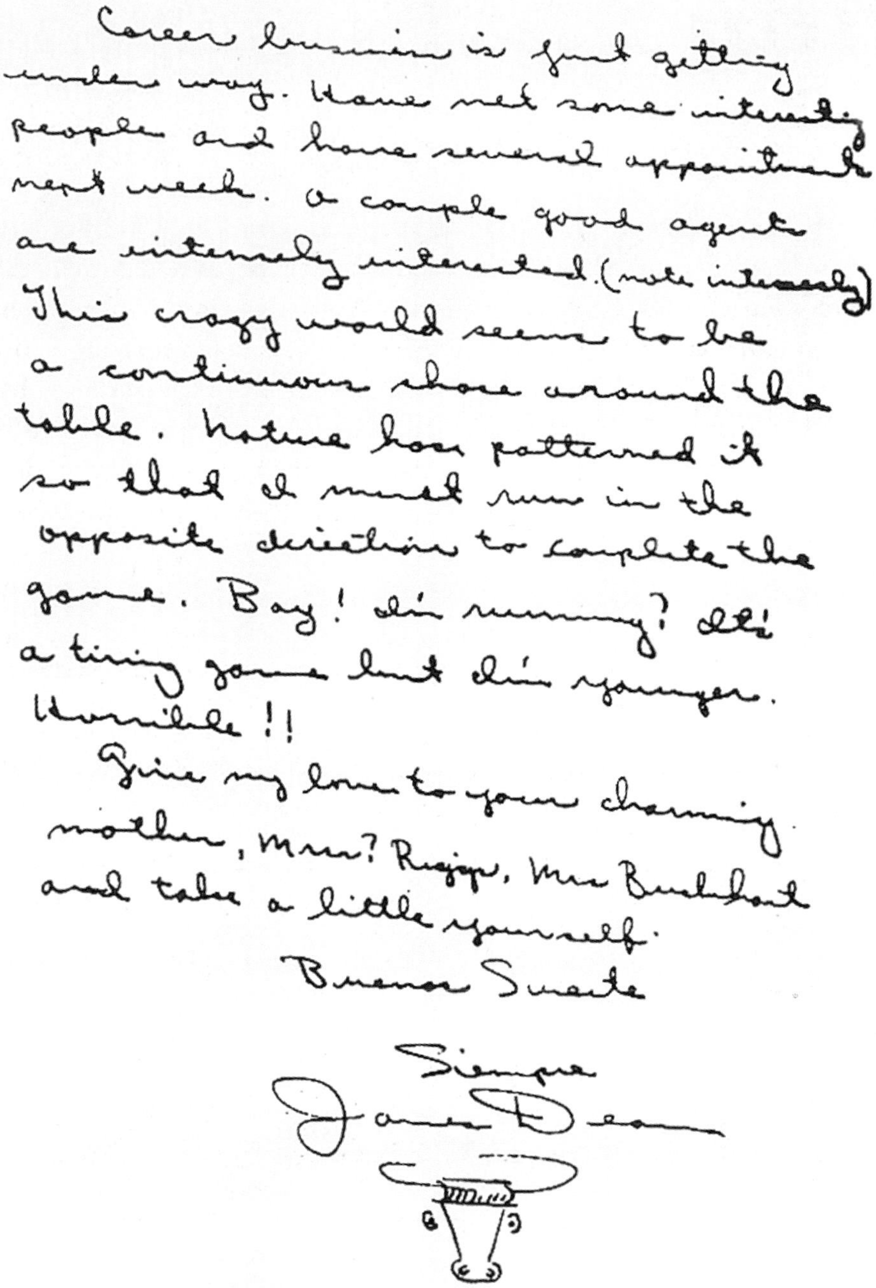

Extract from a letter written by James Dean

.... Career business is just getting under way. Have met some interesting people and have several appointments next week. A couple good agents are intensely interested (note intensely). This crazy world seems to be a continuous chase around the table. Nature has patterned it so that I must run in the opposite direction to complete the game. Boy! I'm running? It's a tiring game but I'm younger. Horrible!!

Give my love to your charming mother, Mrs? Rigger (?), Mrs Buckhart and take a little yourself.

Buenos Suerte.

Siempre James Dean

Diana

PRINCESS OF WALES (1961–1997)

Diana Spencer was born into the English aristocracy. She grew up to become a nursery school teacher, and in 1981 married Prince Charles. The older of her two sons, William, will eventually become king of England. As Princess of Wales, Diana found herself in largely unwanted, often intrusive limelight, but also in a position where she could support charities helping the homeless, drug addicts, poor children and AIDS victims. Her marriage, never the fairytale of popular myth, came to an end in 1992 when she and Prince Charles separated. Diana was killed in a car crash in Paris on August 31, 1997.

Personality overview

Diana's handwriting is large and round, with an openness that suggests someone who was always ready for something new and different. While generally friendly, the variable spacing between the words indicates that she was not always consistent socially and could sometimes withdraw unexpectedly. Her emotional nature is seen in the loose rhythm, so she was quick to express how she felt and would laugh or cry quite readily. However, the upright slant, which is taught in British school models, provides some control over her emotions. She was able to wait for the appropriate time, so long as an emotion was not too strong.

Relationships

The soft, released rhythm in rounded handwriting reflects a profound need to be loved, as well as to love. If a person withdrew their affection, it was probably devastating for Diana. The nonexistent upper zone suggests the lack of a close relationship with her father in childhood, resulting in a continual search for father-replacements later in life. The curved initial strokes also indicate that she looked to old friends for help and support when it was needed.

Intellectual forces

Diana was a concrete thinker who learned best by relating new concepts to what she already knew. The emphasis on the middle zone at the expense of the upper zone reveals a greater interest in people and things than in ideas. Philosophical discussion would probably have bored her, but when the topic turned to more practical applications her interest could be aroused.

Physical drives

The lower zone is moderately long but open, which speaks of strong physical drives, not entirely satisfied. Her private hopes and dreams were left unfulfilled. The round writing style is called an oral writing, and is often seen in the handwriting of women with eating disorders.

Motivating forces

Diana was motivated by a need to serve those she loved. Although the large overall size indicates someone who could also be quite demanding when it came to getting her own needs met, it was easier for her to give of herself than to ask for what she wanted. Her signature is congruent with the text of the writing, telling us that she did not try to hide her real self.

Between the lines

A lower zone made in the form of a large hook, called a cradle, can be seen in Diana's handwriting. As the name implies, this type of lower zone is made by a writer who has not resolved issues surrounding their childhood. The movement to the left signifies "searching for mother." The writer's mother may have been present physically, but he or she missed out on some of what mothering represents, such as love, nurturing, security, and warmth.

A card written by Princess Diana

To dearest Jamie

It's lovely to know that you're now at home & I hope that you and your family will be able to come and see me very soon but until then lots of love from

Diana

Charles Dickens

BRITISH AUTHOR (1812–1870)

Emotionally scarred as a child when forced into a workhouse after his father was sent to debtor's prison, Charles Dickens later used that awful experience in some of his most famous literary works, including *David Copperfield* (1850) and *Great Expectations* (1861). He began his writing career as a freelance reporter in 1829 and went on to write the *Pickwick Papers* (1837), which made him famous. Editor, journalist, and novelist, he produced an impressive body of work including numerous classics. Against doctor's orders, Dickens continued to travel and do public readings until his death.

Personality overview

Dickens' handwriting has a wonderful, flowing rhythm within a speedy script, which indicates a mature integration of the various aspects of his life experiences. He was a man of grace and style, as well as sensitivity, as seen in the moderate variations of middle-zone size and in the well-developed upper zone. The literary *d* also appears in his script, a sign of a natural writer.

Relationships

The moderate right slant reveals emotional response, but also emotional control. Add to that the wide spaces between words and the de-emphasized lower zone, yet strong degree of connectedness between letters, and we see a conflict. Dickens was someone who needed to feel connected with others, but who could not tolerate too much closeness. He would be an amusing companion so long as he was given space. Otherwise he would likely do something to create emotional distance, such as starting an argument, as seen in the downward-slanting *t*-crosses.

Intellectual forces

The tall upper zone and creative connections into this zone indicate Dickens' strong interest in mental activity.

He had a keen mind and could move rapidly from one idea to another. Using a combination of logic, as seen in the ability to connect several letters together, and intuition, found in the open, clear arrangement, he was able to lucidly express the many ideas that filled his head.

Physical drives

The harmonious writing movement—with well-proportioned zones, strong left-to-right movement, and firm pressure—indicates good stamina and vitality. While the emphasis is on the intellect rather than the physical, material world, the warm, colorful ductus (writing line) suggests a sensuous individual with a deep capacity for romance and intimacy.

Motivating forces

Dickens' signature is large and illegible, a far cry from the text of the sample. This demonstrates a very different public character compared to his private persona, which is far more modest. The man he showed to the world was ultimately self-confident and proud. The simplicity of the text, however, tells us that, inside, he was comfortable with who he was and was more concerned with altruistic pursuits than self-aggrandizement.

Between the lines

Your signature is a reflection of what you want the world to know about you. Your first name reveals how you feel about yourself in comparison to how you feel about your family (or your husband's family), as seen in the writing of your surname. An easily read signature, clear and open, congruent with the body of writing, says "what you see is what you get." An illegible signature, such as Dickens', especially one that is also encircled, suggests that the writer has something to hide.

An extract of a letter from Dickens to writer and editor William Harrison Ainsworth

... Foster's situation. I have desired an amanuensis in the Eastern apartment marvellously busy in making extracts of which I suspect there will be no lack. Isn't it a pity that so clever a fellow should not give himself a white flag play. Knowing as he must that there are 20 people eagerly watching for an opportunity to attack him?

A word in your ear. Macready objected to ...'s play—declined it in fact; whereupon ... grew fierce and Macready more manageable and less manageriable, so it is to be done next after a new 5 act play now in the Dales.

Always my dear Ainsworth.

Most faithfully yours,

Charles Dickens

Emily Dickinson

AMERICAN POET (1830–1886)

Emily Dickinson was born in Amherst, Massachusetts. Although they did not have a close relationship with either of their parents, she and her younger sister, Lavinia, lived in the family home all their lives, while their older brother lived next door after his marriage to a friend of Emily's. Neither Emily nor her sister ever married. Dickinson began to write her poetry of rhythms and rhymes around the age of 20, but with the exception of just a handful of pieces, most of her work was not published until after her death. By 1870 Dickinson dressed only in white, saw few visitors, and never left home.

Personality overview

Dickinson's handwriting changed over the years to become highly idiosyncratic in style, more resembling shorthand. This may have been due partly to vision problems. The extreme rightward slant of the letters shows strong responsiveness. However, the disturbed picture of space and oversimplification of form echo her isolation. Thus, the wide spacing between letters and words provide a defense against an intensely emotional nature.

Relationships

Another aspect of an extreme right slant is a profound need for affection and emotional display in someone who could easily become carried away with her feelings. Feeling unable to make social connections as easily in person, she poured her emotions into her poetry and letters. The many rolled strokes in the middle zone are a sign of self-involvement, and extremely wide spaces between letters and words reveal an inability to connect with the outside world and make emotional bonds.

Intellectual forces

The overall linear quality, showing intellectual orientation, is somewhat at odds with the rounded forms, which signify an emotional nature. A conflict between mind and heart exists. Dickinson had a utilitarianism that allowed her to stick to the basics, eliminating whatever went beyond the bare essentials. Yet, while a wealth of ideas flooded her mind, she had trouble concentrating for long periods. The slashed *i*-dots are the mark of a sharp, sometimes acerbic, wit.

Physical drives

The apparently light pressure, lack of connections, and words falling down, suggest depression. There is not much physical stamina in this disintegrated writing and the remarkably long *t*-crossings show that her energy came in bursts. The oversimplification is also a sign of someone who was too stimulated by what was going on around her to burden herself with anything more.

Motivating forces

The writing movement is essentially centripetal, toward the self. There is no relationship in these unusual forms to the school models of the time, revealing Dickinson's independent nature and need to create something of her own. At the same time, the strong degree of disconnectedness, wide spaces, and illegibility, reflect one who was emotionally detached and unconcerned with whether or

Between the lines

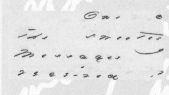

Rolled in or spiral strokes move in a centripetal direction, toward the center or back to self. There are many such strokes in Dickinson's script. In the middle zone they suggest egocentrism and selfishness, while on final strokes they indicate retreat from the social world. In the lower zone, self-centeredness in sexual activities is likely. Rolled initial strokes in the upper zone signify vanity and presumption.

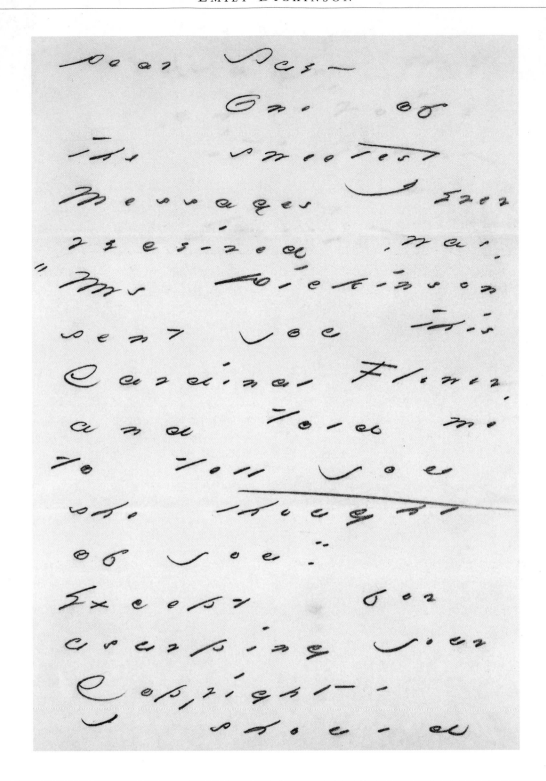

An extract from a letter written by Emily Dickinson, probably to her sister

Dear Sister (?)
One of the sweetest messages I ever received was "Miss Dickinson sent you this Cardinal Flower and told me to tell you she thought of you."
Except for escaping (?) your Copyright.
I should ....

Amelia Earhart

AMERICAN AVIATOR (1897–1937)

Kansan Amelia Earhart worked as a nurse and a social worker before taking up flying against her family's wishes. In 1928 she published her first book detailing her experiences as the first woman to fly across the Atlantic, albeit only as a passenger. Four years later she crossed the Atlantic solo from Newfoundland to Ireland in record time, and was soon making regular flights across the United States. After completing two-thirds of a planned flight around the world with navigator Fred Noonan, Earhart's plane vanished over the Pacific Ocean on July 2 (?), 1937.

Personality overview

Earhart's handwriting cries for freedom and wide open spaces. Not just the arrangement but the words themselves are spread out, giving the impression of a vivacious, carefree person who refused to be hemmed in. She demanded elbow room, though the loose garlands show her demands would be made in the friendliest possible way. The writing is simple and unpretentious, a reflection of her character. Earhart could not be bothered putting on airs, but had a naturalness of expression and an impatience to get on with things.

Relationships

Although the garlands tell us this was a person who cared about others, the wide spacing in the lines, words, and letters reflect little need for social contact. There is a high degree of connectedness, so a certain amount of inter-action would have been important, but overall she was a better observer than a participant when it came to social-izing. Earhart was quite happy with her own company, which undoubtedly served her well on long solo flights.

Intellectual forces

There is plenty of activity in the upper zone and the writing is quite simplified, indicating intelligence and the ability to think fast without a lot of preparatory details. Quick to see cause and effect, Earhart was a fast learner who could put what she learned to instant use. She could also handle several tasks at once without becoming confused, able to move easily back and forth between one activity and another.

Physical drives

Although it is goal-directed, there is also a restless quality about the handwriting that suggests a person who enjoyed change. Nonetheless, while there is energy present, it is of a more intellectual nature, as seen in the high-crossed *t*-bars and light pressure of the sample. Earhart was probably more comfortable using her mind than her body in most areas of her life.

Motivating forces

The need for space and freedom are uppermost in Earhart's writing. The *t*'s crossed at the very tops indicate ambition. The crosses are also long, so she was willing to pour in whatever was needed in order to attain her goals. With the light pressure it seems likely that, once she met her objectives, Earhart would probably have needed to take some time off to recoup her energy, as her stamina was not all that great.

Between the lines

One of the major connective forms is the garland, which is the shape of a cupped hand or a bowl. Natural, open garlands such as those used by Earhart are made by people with a "live and let live" attitude. Open from the top, they are a sign of receptivity and friendliness. Writers who use this connective form are sociable and open, and are seldom interested in controlling or trying to control others.

A letter from Earhart to Ruth (?)

February 9, 1930

Dear Ruth (?)

The enclosed is a sample of what I did not think would happen.

I saw Glad (?) in California and shall tell you her reactions.

A.E.

Thomas Edison

AMERICAN INVENTOR (1847–1931)

Thomas Alva Edison was born in Milan, Ohio, the youngest of seven children. He was a poor student at school partly due to an undiagnosed hearing problem, yet, as an adult, he became the foremost inventor of his day. Edison was only 10 years old when he set up his first laboratory in his father's basement. After working as a telegrapher, Edison moved to New York in 1869 to concentrate on inventing. He went on to patent more than 1,000 inventions and is credited with inventing the electric lightbulb, the phonograph, the Edison storage battery, the electric pen, the mimeograph, and the first motion picture projector.

Personality overview

Edison's handwriting combines strength and flexibility. The chief connective form is the garland, an adaptable, open form that illustrates one who is receptive and willing to listen. He had the capacity to make quick changes of direction and to try new methods when old ones were no longer working. On the other hand, the long, strong *t*-crosses are made by someone who had no difficulty giving orders, and the upright slant provides additional strength to the garlands.

Relationships

Some words have many breaks between letters, while others have a greater degree of connection. In some cases one word even connects to another, an indication of fluid thinking. Socially, though, Edison could not be counted on for consistency. He had a great deal of charm, but if an idea came into his head, he would abruptly turn on his heel and be gone.

Intellectual forces

Edison's neat, well-organized handwriting reflects an organized mind. The spaces between words, letters, and lines are clear, which is a sign of an ability to see the big picture but also to keep all the constituent parts in their proper perspective. There is a moderate amount of simplification in the writing, so he was able to go to the heart of the matter without the need for a lot of extraneous details. Edison also left room for intuition, which could burst through the smooth breaks at the baseline and blossom in the middle zone.

Physical drives

There is energy in the smooth, rapid movement. The narrow margins suggest one who filled his time with plenty of activity. The flat tops on the letter *r* are a sign of one who worked well with tools. The lower zone is mixed in length and width, and some downstrokes tend to thin out, so it would have been important for Edison to get enough rest, or his stamina might have given out.

Motivating forces

Motivated by creativity, Edison's handwriting has original, simplified forms, as well as what are called cultural letters. These are the Greek *e* and the lyrical *d*, which is also a Greek form of the letter. Greek letters are often used by writers and poets, and others who have a propensity for original thinking.

Between the lines

The degree to which a writer connects one letter to another reveals, among other things, how much personal contact he or she needs. A high degree of connectedness is adopted by those who enjoy a lot of interpersonal communication and close contact with other people. Many breaks between letters, on the other hand, is a sign that a person has some degree of difficulty with social interaction. In Edison's case, the degree of connectedness is quite mixed.

A letter written by Thomas Edison to Jay Gould in 1877

Jan. 20 1877
Jay Gould Esq.

  Dear Sir

  Mr. Eckert does not want me to be connected with the A&P. It was not necessary that a man should be knocked down and have a fact forced down his throat with a crow-bar, there are many other and gentler methods, for instance, keep an impatient man like myself waiting 3 weeks to decide about removing a partition, causing me to wait for days and weeks for small sums due, doubting my honesty in a transaction of four dollars, urging me to produce things and then refuse to pay for them, granting no money to conduct experiments, and then say I am not doing anything for the Co. In fact conducting his business with me in a manner that it was one long lingering disappointment. I have never complained but once or twice to you in these two years, ...

Albert Einstein

German-Born Mathematician (1879–1955)

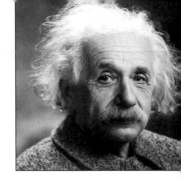

Albert Einstein, born in Germany, was just 16 when he began to formulate his special theory of relativity. International fame struck in 1919 when the general theory of relativity, an explanation of the fundamental laws of the universe, overthrew the Newtonian physics that had dominated until then. Awarded the Nobel prize in 1921, Einstein found himself increasingly at risk in Germany as the Nazis rose to power and moved to Princeton in 1933, later taking U.S. citizenship. A supporter of the creation of a Jewish state in Israel, Einstein also continued his work on general relativity and other theories until his death.

Personality overview

The picture of space is emphasized in the very compact arrangement, with narrow line and word spacing. This shows that Einstein preferred to allow things to work out as they developed, rather than being tightly planned and organized. Lack of adequate space interferes with a clear perspective. However, it appears that he had a lot to say and was anxious to get his thoughts across. The capital letters are simple, indicating simple pride and a reluctance to draw attention to himself.

Relationships

Basically conventional, being part of a group would have given Einstein a sense of security. He was clearly willing to adapt to various circumstances and to the people around him, although there is the possibility that some-one who needed a lot of space would have felt crowded by him. The page represents the environment, so another facet of the crowded spatial arrangement is that it is adopted by a person who needs be in charge of his surroundings. He must control all the space on the page.

Intellectual forces

Einstein's handwriting reveals a quick thinker with the ability to string together a series of concepts in logical succession. The upper and lower zones are fairly well balanced but the middle zone is neglected, with many letters fading into threads. In addition the page is only moderately organized, showing that he put little emphasis on planning his everyday life. Clearly mundane activities paled into insignificance when Einstein was involved in more interesting pursuits, such as working on his laws and theories.

Physical drives

There is a great deal of movement in the writing, and the narrow margins on both sides of the page signify a busy, impatient person who could hardly wait to get going on projects that intrigued him. Einstein was uncomfortable if he had a lot of free time on his hands, as he needed to be active and involved all the time. This is reinforced by words at the ends of lines, which have their very long, final strokes. Even when he could have left a little space in his life, Einstein chose not to.

Motivating forces

Einstein's handwriting shows that he was mainly motivated by his need to be productive. It is significant that what he actually produced was so important and affected the course of history.

Between the lines

Velocity, or speed of writing, relates to the writer's level of intelligence, spontaneity, and ability to take action. It shows how reflexively the writer approaches life and how rapidly he or she thinks. Slow writing is not necessarily a sign of low intelligence, although extremely slow writing often is. Einstein wrote quickly and fast writing is always done by fast thinkers, which implies intelligence.

Part of Einstein's explanation of his theory of relativity, written in 1912

... tends towards infinity, when y nears the value of c, it requires therefore, an infinite expenditure of Energy for the body to reach c. To see that ... expression becomes that for Newton's mechanics for small speeds, we develop ... the denominator (after ... with ...) and obtain:

EL = mc² + m/2y² + ... (28)

The second term on the right hand side is the ... expression for the constant energy of classical mechanics. What is the meaning of the first term that is independent of y? This has, however strongly ..., as we have arbitrarily omitted an additive constant in (28). But conversely, a look at 28 shows us that the term mc² is inextricably connected with the second ... m/2 y². One already tends at this point therefore, to give the term in c² a real meaning, to look at it as (the expression for) the energy of the resting point. Following this interpretation we have a body of the ... mass ... as an energy ... of the value mc² ... ("resting-energy" of the body). We can change the resting energy of a body, for example if we ... it heat. If, therefore, mc², instead of the resting energy of the body ... equal ...

Elizabeth I

QUEEN OF ENGLAND (1533–1603)

Often remembered as the Virgin Queen, Elizabeth I was born the daughter of Henry VIII and Anne Boleyn. After much religious and political intrigue she became queen of England in 1558. Well known for her strength and courage, she famously declared in a speech calling her troops to action against Spain, "I know I have the body of a weak and feeble woman, but I have the heart and stomach of a king; and a king of England, too." Her reign saw England's asserting itself as a major political and commercial power, and a flowering of literature and the arts.

Personality overview

The writing style of Elizabeth's time was quite different from styles today, but we can still glean important information from her script. There is a tremendous amount going on in her handwriting. The flourishes are somewhat self-important, which is hardly surprising in one of her rank. Yet, if we look beneath these the writing is quite simplified, with a thready quality that attests to a high intelligence. The movement to the right and steady margins are a testament to one who looked to the future with hope and courage.

Relationships

Elizabeth was not one to commit easily. The high degree of threadiness, coupled with the many breaks within words, reveal a need to stay free, ready to change direction at a moment's notice. At the same time, the strong picture of movement in the writing indicates a woman of fierce emotions who could, from time to time, erupt into impulsive behavior.

Intellectual forces

The writing is very fast, considering its elaborate style. Elizabeth could make quick decisions based on her intuitive reactions to situations. The indefinite character of the middle zone suggests that she was less interested in the details of a matter than the bottom line, so she may have jumped to conclusions too quickly, without the benefit of all the facts.

Physical drives

The focus in this handwriting is on activity and movement. The spatial arrangement is rather crowded, not just because of the many flourished strokes but because the space left between the lines is narrow. This is generally the sign of a very busy person who tries to pack as much as she can into each moment. A loss of perspective can be expected when someone is more concerned with acting than planning.

Motivating forces

Elizabeth's signature is large and showy, as was the style of the day, giving it a bearing of pomp and circumstance. The large capital letters in the script indicate a strong sense of self in a woman who did not hesitate to express her opinions. Her strong pride in herself and her accomplishments impelled her to continually move forward to ever greater achievement.

Between the lines

There is no set rule for how much space should be left between lines, but graphologists agree that the amount of space the writer leaves provides information about how that person schedules his or her life and time, and how they use their resources. Very narrow line spacing, as seen here, is a sign of reduced mental clarity, whereas extremely wide line spacing indicates a lack of spontaneity. As with all other aspects of handwriting analysis, balance is the key.

A letter written by Queen Elizabeth I to Henry IV of France

Queen Elizabeth was a prolific writer of speeches, poems, and letters. She usually wrote in English, but this letter is in her own phonetic version of French. Henry III, king of Navarre in France's extreme southwest, succeeded to the French throne as King Henry IV 1589. He promised to be a strong Protestant ally for Elizabeth in mainland Europe, but his conversion to Catholicism in 1593 profoundly shocked and alienated the English monarch.

Duke Ellington

AMERICAN MUSICIAN (1899–1974)

Born Edward Kennedy Ellington in Washington, D.C., bandleader and pianist Duke Ellington went on to become one of the most influential figures in jazz history. After studying piano from an early age, Ellington began playing professionally at 17. In the early 1920s, at the Kentucky Club in New York, he formed the group that later became the core of his legendary band. Known as one of the founders of big-band jazz, Ellington is also famed for his innovative groupings of instruments, for composing music that drew out unique sounds, and for orchestrating more than 1,000 pieces, including film scores, operas, and ballets.

Personality overview

Ellington's handwriting is filled with excitement and movement. This is someone who saw life as a party to be enjoyed and shared with others. The strongly released rhythm attests to an emotionally active person who had no choice but to express himself. The dynamic horizontal movement in the upper zone, seen in the long *t*-crosses and dashed *i*-dots, reveals one who was comfortable directing others. However, he could also be rather tyrannical about getting his own way, as illustrated by some of the *t*-crosses pointing downward, making the *t* resemble an *x*, and also by the tall extensions on the *p*'s and the many sharply angled letters.

Relationships

The close letters, lines, and words point to a highly sociable person whose witty, charming manner undoubtedly brought him many friends. In addition, the generally looped style and the variable size of the middle zone are indicators of sensitivity and the ability to understand things outside his own experience. Thready forms such as Ellington's are also the hallmark of a person who has a talent for talking to others on their own level, adapting to whoever happens to be present at the time, whether they are a janitor or king.

Intellectual forces

Here was someone who enjoyed visualizing his various plans and schemes before putting them into practice. With the open upper zone and original letter forms, Ellington had a superb imagination and the ability to see in his mind's eye all the possibilities in what lay ahead. Using his considerable intuition, he was also able instantly to understand how new information could fit in with what he already knew, and how to best make use of it.

Physical drives

The impulsive writing movement in a strongly released rhythm is a sign of low self-discipline, of someone who acts in the moment without thinking about the consequences. However, the maturity in the simplified, original, well-developed forms suggests Ellington's innate common sense helped him make good decisions.

Motivating forces

The released writing shows that Ellington would not have participated in anything for long unless it was fun to do. Drawn to a wide spectrum of experiences, he probably never did the same thing twice in the same way. The elegant simplicity of the script also indicates sophistication in both his personal presentation and his work.

Between the lines

Rhythm in handwriting is determined by the balance of contraction and release. A released rhythm such as Ellington's has an emphasis on rightward movement and signifies one who is emotionally expressive and highly sensitive to everything in his or her environment. Release is seen in simplified, often thready forms, in speed, and in a tendency toward a loopy writing style that is more rounded than linear.

A page of Duke Ellington's handwritten notes

SOUND or NOISE AGREEABLE TO THE EAR

Music is the Natural Subject.

Jazz is the Banner under which I have Performed & I'm ... of the Fact that I Don't Really think in an Honest Flag(?)—the Word Jazz is ... Grossly Exaggerated—Over Emphasized Over used & applyed in Too Many Directions I Could Very Well Understand the Confusion & Frustration of—Say—a man arrived today From the Moon & Said—I want to Hear Jazz—... (RECORDS) Would We Play for Him Louie—...—Diz—Kenton—Miles & Hawk, Jelly Roll—Tatum & the Lion, Jas P. Fats, Bird—...—Lombado—the Dorseys, Glenn Mills, Whiteman(?), Mancini, Henderson, Coltrane, Ella—Joe Turner—Django—Brubeck—Rich, Edna Stravinsky (?) wrote for Woody

All of these are great names. Claimed By Jazz—Some from the Conservatory—Some Have just applied Themselves to God given Talent & as a ... Established a ... in the Hall of Jazz Fame—But What is it about all of them that ... one imaginary (?) category (They said go) (good music)—All Individuals—If Jazz Means anything (IT IS) Freedom of Expression...

William Faulkner

AMERICAN WRITER (1897–1962)

William Faulkner, a high school dropout, went on to become one of America's best-known writers, with novels such as *As I Lay Dying* (1930) and *Absalom Absalom!* (1936). Many of his books were set in the fictional Jefferson and Yoknapatawpha County, which were patterned after his own home in Oxford, Mississippi. Faulkner was an intensely private person yet, after being awarded the Nobel Prize for Literature in 1950, he became a goodwill ambassador for the State Department. After struggling with alcoholism for much of his life, Faulkner died of a heart attack aged 64.

Personality overview

The minuscule writing validates Faulkner's extreme need for privacy. While the overall size is tiny, the middle zone width is in good proportion to the height, indicating self-confidence and assurance. Combine the small size, upright slant, and print-script style, and objectivity and a sense of realism become key characteristics. This is someone who, once he became involved in a task or project, would thoroughly immerse himself, to the exclusion of all else around him.

Relationships

Faulkner's interests were directed inward rather than toward other people. He would undoubtedly be very loyal to those close to him, but otherwise worked best on his own. The close letter spacing indicates that he was not so much aloof as he was self-interested. Writing this small can also be a sign of depression or emotional instability in one who has great difficulty in dealing with day-to-day life. Such a writer feels the need to withdraw, or escape. Faulkner himself created his own world in his writing.

Intellectual forces

The small, upright printing reveals someone who made decisions based more on his head than his heart. His thinking style was logical, and he communicated his thoughts directly, with no frills. The simplicity goes to an extreme, as he fails to cross any *t*'s or *f*'s, except for capital letters. While in some writing this would indicate procrastination or carelessness, in Faulkner's case it may be more an affectation considering other aspects of his writing that contradict this first interpretation.

Physical drives

The apparently thick strokes (multi-generation copies may have increased the appearance of heaviness) are often made by those who indulge in excesses of various kinds. The ink flows onto the paper without restraint, impairing legibility. In the same way, the writer's inner drives spill out and overtake him. The wide left margin suggests a need to flee from some traumatic past event(s) that he had so far been unable resolve, as shown by the lack of return strokes in the lower zone.

Motivating forces

Another facet of pastosity (thick strokes) is impression-ability. The writer thinks in images and soaks up sensuous experiences. Faulkner had the ability to translate those images onto paper in order to express what he could not say aloud.

---

*the curling llowen spaces, I could
I passed whene T.P. was leaning
: and hil again and went in along the*

Between the lines

Extremes in handwriting, such as the small size of Faulkner's writing, immediately draw the eye. Other extremes include extra length or width, heavy pressure, letters slanting so far to the right or left that they nearly fall over, and overly ornamental forms. Extremes are a form of compensation, where the writer draws your attention away from where he or she feels inadequate by exaggerating somewhere else.

Twilight   April 7, 1928

Through the fence, between the curling flower spaces, I could see them hitting. Then they came on toward where the flag was and I went along the fence. I passed where T.P. was leaning against the flower fence. Then they stopped hitting where the flag was and she went to the table and hit again and went in. ~~along the~~ I went along beside the fence and T.P. came away from the flower fence.

"Here, Caddy," ~~one of~~ one of them said.

The boy came to him and ~~the man took~~ then he hit again and went along the fence. Then the fence stopped and I held to it and watched them go away.

"Hush up that moaning," T.P. said. "They'll be some more coming by in a minute." They went on away, hitting again.

"Hush it up, now," T.P. said. So I hushed, and went back along the fence to where the flag was.

"Come on," T.P. said. "Let go down to the branch, where they playing."

I held to the fence and watched the flag, and the pasture.

"Shut up that moaning," T.P. said. "~~If they won't~~ I can't make them come back just for you to watch them. Come on, lets go down to the branch. Maybe we can find me they balls. Here. Here they is. Way over yonder. Look." It came to the fence and pointed through it. "See them? They aint coming back here. Come on, now."

We went along the fence and came to the other fence, where our shadows were. My shadow was higher up the fence than Luster's. ~~We~~ We came to the broken place and went through it.

"~~Wait," Caddy said. "You're caught on a nail." She uncaught me and we crawled through.~~

"Wait a minute," Luster said. "You caught on that nail again. Cant you never crawl through this place without snapping on that nail?"

Caddy uncaught me and we crawled through. "Uncle Maury said to not let anybody see us, so we better stoop over. Stoop over, Benjy. Like this, see?" We stooped over and crossed the garden, where the flowers rasped and rattled against us. The ground was hard. We climbed the fence, where the pigs were grunting and snuffing. The ground was hard.

A manuscript page from Faulkner's novel *The Sound and The Fury*, page 1

Twilight April 7 1928
  Through the fence, between the curling flower spaces, I could see them hitting. There they came on toward where the flag was and I went along the fence. I passed where T.P. was leaning against the flower fence. Then they stopped hitting where the flag was and she went to the table and hit again and went in. I went along beside the fence and T.P. came away from the flower fence.
  "Here, Caddy," one of them said.
  The boy came to him and then he hit again and went along the fence. Then the fence stopped and I held to it and watched them go away.
  "Hush up that moaning," T.P. said. "They'll be some more coming back in a minute." They went away, hitting again.
  "Hush it up, now," T.P. said. So I hushed, and went back along the fence to where the flag was.
  "Come on," T.P. said, "lets go down to the ..., where they playing."
  I held to the fence and watched the flag, and the pasture.
  "Shut up that moaning," T.P. said. I can't make them come back just for you to watch them. Come on, ... (continued)

F. Scott Fitzgerald

AMERICAN NOVELIST (1896–1940)

Francis Scott Fitzgerald was an American novelist and writer of short stories famed for his depictions of the 1920s Jazz Age. After attending Princeton University he joined the army, and in 1918 met his future wife Zelda Sayre. His life with her was spoken of almost as much as his novels. In 1925, while living on the French Riviera, Fitzgerald completed his best known work, *The Great Gatsby*. However, by 1930 he was drinking heavily and Zelda had a mental breakdown from which she never recovered. Fitzgerald spent his final years living quietly, but died of a heart attack aged just 44.

Personality overview

There is a romantic character to the soft garlands that grace Fitzgerald's handwriting, these being the form of someone willing to adapt and cooperate with others. The garlands are also the mark of a caring individual who could be vulnerable to abuse. Yet, while his sensitivity to the pain of others would make it hard for him to say no, the emphasis on the up/down movement, which has a self-protective element, and the strokes that return to the self, rather than moving rightward, show that, while he generally preferred to keep the peace, Fitzgerald was not a total pushover.

Relationships

This charming writing attests to the sophistication and social polish required to develop and maintain meaningful relationships with a variety of personality types. The dark color, yet lack of heavy pressure, reveal that Fitzgerald was an easygoing person with a relaxed attitude, while the softness of the form reveals an avoidance of conflict.

Intellectual forces

Although plenty of attention is also given to the practical details, the garlands are an open cup, ready to receive information from intuition. The well-spaced page, meanwhile, reflects organized thinking in one who was adept at planning ahead. Fitzgerald's ability to produce an original writing style also shows his capacity to put things together in new, imaginative ways, after carefully evaluating and considering the many aspects of the subject at hand.

Physical drives

Fitzgerald's senses were finely tuned to line, form, and color. At his best in a tranquil environment where beauty and harmony prevailed, anything less could damage his physical and emotional health. In this rather thick, pastose writing we also see an appreciation for the good life. This type of person needs more of everything that touches his or her senses: more food, more wine, more spices. The writer clearly relished experiences for the pure sensual feeling he received from them.

Motivating forces

Image was important to Fitzgerald, as the writing is carefully executed and the picture of form is highly developed. The regular, original style implies that he was very much motivated by the need to express his creativity in the context of love and romance.

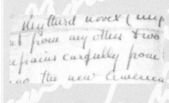

Between the lines

Writers like Fitzgerald adopt a carefully constructed form of writing known as "persona writing." Rather than a free-flowing, natural script, persona handwriting has an artistic look, almost as if it were drawn. This writing style does not permit much spontaneity because the writer spends a lot of time making things look just right.

A letter written by Fitzgerald to Mr. Baldwin

... B. 1896, Sept 24th in St. Paul, Miss. Spent early years travelling all over America, living for a while in Sarycuse & for a while in Buffalo. My first reading was composed entirely of Henty, Alger & Ralph Henry Barber. The authors who influenced me were Captain McKenzie & Wells. (See This Side of the ... which treats all this very fully, being to a great extent autobiographical).

My third novel (unpublished) is just finished & quite different from the other two in that it is an attempt at farce and refrains carefully from trying to "hit anything off"—five years ago the new American novels needed comment by the author because they were facing a public that had had very little but trash for a hundred years—that is to say the exceptions were few and far between and most of them commercial failures. But now that there is an intelligent body of opinion guided by such men as McKenzie, Edmund Wilson and Van Wyke Brookes comments should be unnecessary. The writer, if he has any aspirations toward art, should try to convey the feel of his scenes, places and people directly—as Conrad does, as a few Americans, notably Willa Cather are already trying to do.

I am a pessimist, a communist (with Nietchean overtones) with no hobbies except conversation, and I'm trying to repress that. My enthusiasms at present include Stravinski, ... Braun, Mencken, Conrad, Joyce, the early Gertrude Stein, ... and all books about that period which lies between the ... and 13th centuries.

Most sincerely,

F. Scott Fitzgerald

Benjamin Franklin

AMERICAN INVENTOR AND DIPLOMAT

(1706–1790)

Benjamin Franklin—author, publisher, scientist, and inventor—is probably best known for his role as an emissary of the American colonies to Britain and for helping to draft both the Declaration of Independence and the U.S. Constitution. Born in Boston he started out in the printing trade and later went into publishing. By the time he began his diplomatic career in 1757, he had invented the Franklin stove and the lightning rod, and his experiments with electricity are legendary. Later accomplishments of Franklin's included promoting the establishment of a fire department, a library, and a university in Pennsylvania.

Personality overview

This sample was written when Franklin was 71, and reveals a man who was still vital and energetic. The rhythm is smooth and elastic, with a harmonious symmetry between contraction and release. The high degree of regularity indicates self-discipline and an orderly lifestyle. The capital letters are large and ordinary for the time, and his signature is plain and legible, showing the unpretentious manner of a self-confident individualist.

Relationships

The high degree of connectedness between letters, along with the strong right slant and moderate spaces between words, reveal an amiable, compassionate person for whom social contact was an important part of life. The good humor and composure in the even pace across the page reflect Franklin's appreciation for communication with others. The pastose flow of ink also shows a warm personality who was quite fond of his creature comforts.

Intellectual forces

There is an emphasis on upper-zone activities in the tall, moderately open upper loops—Franklin's busy mind had a strong interest in intellectual pursuits. Exploring new areas and understanding what made things work was a driving force. The well-organized page also indicates his ability to plan and schedule his activities and accomplish a great deal from day to day. The lyrical *d* that appears in his writing was part of the school model of his day, but often reflects someone with poetic leanings.

Physical drives

The balance between the zones in a picture of strong rhythm suggests vitality and stamina. Although Franklin suffered from poor health at the end of his life, at the time of this writing he had energy enough to accomplish whatever he wanted. There is a practicality in the smooth left-to-right movement, as the letters always return to the baseline. This shows a pragmatic way of operating.

Motivating forces

The tall upper zone, well-formed capitals, and excellent rhythm show that Franklin was motivated by his need to lead others. His self-confidence, seen in the firm, rapid arcade connections and the forward movement, are a sign of courage and fortitude in the face of challenges.

Between the lines

The letter *d* is considered a personal letter with special significance. The height of the *d* tells how tall the writer feels. Excessive height is a sign of vanity, while a very short *d* is a sign of modesty. An inflated loop signifies extreme sensitivity, and the Greek, or lyrical, *d* of Franklin's script is poetic. Finally there is the maniacal *d*, one that tips over in explosive emotional discharge.

Sir Paris, Aug. 24. 1777

M. de Knobelauch, who will have the Honour of delivering this to you, is recommended to me as an Officer of much Experience, and capable of rendering good Service in our Armies if employ'd. He goes over at his own Expence, & without any Promise from me, as indeed we are not authoris'd to give any. But I beg leave to recommend him to your Excellency's Notice, & to such Employment as you may find is convenient to give him. With great Respect I have the honour to be

Your Excellency's most obed.t humb Serv.t

B Franklin

Gen. Washington

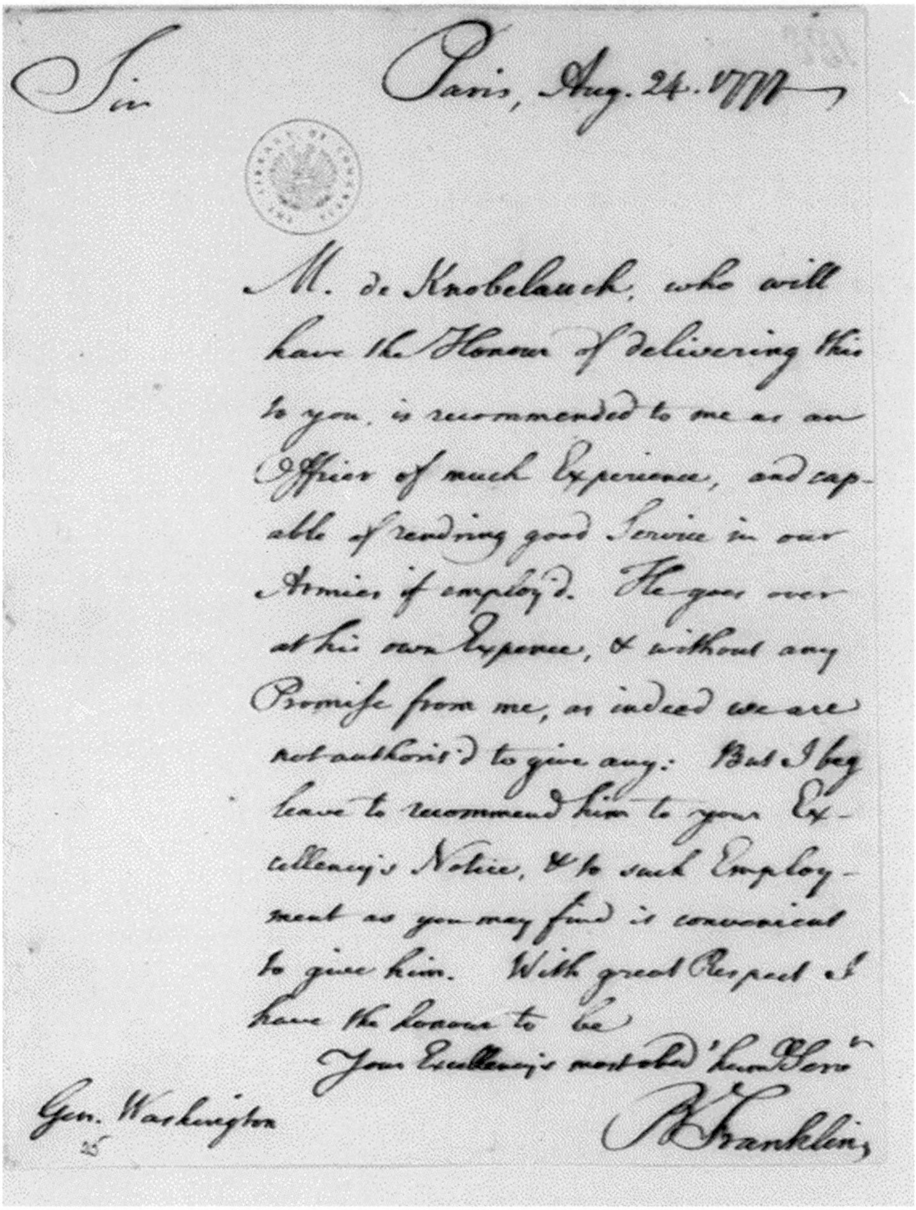

A letter written by Benjamin Franklin to George Washington

Paris, Aug. 24 1777

Sir

M. de Knobelauch (?), who will have the Honour of delivering this to you, is recommended to me as an Officer of much Experience, and capable of rendering good Service in our Armies if employ'd. He goes over at his own Expense, & without any Promise from me, as indeed we are not authoris'd to give any. But I beg leave to recommend him to your Excellency's Notice, & to such Employment as you may find is convenient to give him. With great Respect I have the honour to be

Your Excellency's most obed' humb Serv'

B. Franklin

Sigmund Freud

PSYCHIATRIST (1856–1939)

Sigmund Freud was born Moravia, but lived in Vienna, Austria from an early age. Freud trained as a doctor of medicine, but later became interested in hypnotherapy and dream analysis. He worked for a time at a psychiatric clinic where he developed his theories that mental illness could be caused by purely psychological factors buried deep in the subject's subconscious. He first used the term "psychoanalysis" in 1896, and his own self-analysis began shortly afterward. Although some of his precepts were later rejected, most modern schools of psychiatry have their foundations in Freudian theory.

Personality overview

Freud's handwriting is filled with what he would have called "id energy." The strong movement to the right shows his passion and drive. At the same time, the letters are narrow, which effectively puts the brakes on the movement and produces conflict between the "ego" and the "superego." The changeable size of the middle-zone height demonstrates a mercurial, unpredictable personality. He could promote his ideas with intense enthusiasm, rolling right over anyone who disagreed with him.

Relationships

The dominant form in Freud's handwriting is the angle connecting form, which tells us that he had to be the leader, the master in his relationships. Not one to suffer fools gladly, his impatience, seen in the very hasty speed of the writing, could potentially make life difficult for those around him. The thick, inky strokes are made by a person who could also be overly self-indulgent, allowing his own urges to take precedence over others' desires.

Intellectual forces

The handwriting is linear rather than curved, with a strong upper zone. Combined with the angular connections, this reveals an intellectually oriented person with firm, fixed ideas. When he made quick changes of direction it was not by way of making adaptations. Rather, Freud would rapidly switch from one thought to another and expect everyone to keep up with him. If they did not, they could expect to incur his anger.

Physical drives

Although he had strong physical drives, which we see in the long lower-zone letters, Freud's intellectual energy was the strongest force in his personality. It may be that at the time of writing he was feeling unwell, possibly fatigued or discouraged by some physical ailment. This is shown in the sinuous baseline, with its downward tendency, especially at the ends of lines where he could have chosen to move to the next line, but instead squeezed the words in.

Motivating forces

The emphasis in the writing is on movement, manifesting an ardent, enthusiastic nature. For Freud, a great motivating factor was the need for power and control. He had to be in charge and would not easily follow orders. The angled forms and heavy flow of ink signify a rigid, opinionated personality.

Between the lines

Handwriting consists of three zones—upper, middle and lower—with each symbolizing an area of personality functioning. In Freudian terms the id corresponds to the lower zone, the ego to the middle zone, and the superego to the upper zone. However, no area of personality or handwriting can be properly considered outside the context of the whole personality or the whole handwriting. Each part interacts with all the others to provide a complete picture.

A contents list for *Imago*, a journal edited by Sigmund Freud

1) Two children's lies, 8 small sheets
2) Inquiries into dream meaning, 4 small sheets
3) Concerning ...
4) ...
5) A ... Leonardo da Vinci, 34 big sheets
6) ...
7) Concerning the ...
8) Psychoanalytical remarks about an autobiographical account of Paranoia (Schreber-analysis), 38 sheets
9) Remarks on a case ...

Galileo Galilei

ASTRONOMER, MATHEMATICIAN (1564–1642)

Galileo was born in Pisa, Italy, the eldest son of a merchant and musician. He began studying medicine in 1581, but two years later turned to mathematics and physical sciences. Galileo was the first to explore the sky with an astronomical telescope and collected what was then amazing celestial information. Because he supported the teachings of Copernicus (who theorized that the planets revolve around the sun), Galileo came into conflict with the Catholic church and for the last eight years of his life was under house arrest. However, his writings were translated and widely distributed in other parts of Europe.

Personality overview

Galileo's script has the airy, light quality of a thoughtful, cerebral person whose mind was always ready to explore new ideas. The right margin is narrower than the left, and the overall spacing is clear. Thus, he focused on the future and the possibilities inherent in any situation. The simplified forms and well-developed upper zone are indicative of one who was comfortable bending reality to suit his purposes. That is, he was not satisfied accepting the way things were generally done and understood at the time, but was most assuredly an explorer. With the tall upper zone, he was apparently untroubled when others did not agree with him.

Relationships

Again, the upper-zone emphasis in the handwriting and the small middle zone make it likely that Galileo could get lost in his world of ideas. As a result, personal relationships may have played a secondary role in his life. He could be self-involved to the point that nothing, and no one, else mattered. To other people, he might have seemed cold or uncaring, but the mundane, everyday world would sometimes cease to exist for him he was so wrapped up in thought.

Intellectual forces

The nicely organized page mirrors Galileo's capacity for clear thinking and presentation. He wrote quickly, showing great enthusiasm for his subject matter. The writing is simple, including the capital letters, which tells us that he was intellectually independent. The upper zone, where we find some very tall letters, shows his interest in the theoretical and his desire to increase his knowledge.

Physical drives

Some of Galileo's baselines are concave and others go downhill. This shows that he may have been discouraged at the time of writing, attempting to pull himself up out of a sense of despondency. An air of impatience is also communicated in the fast writing speed, as if he could not get his thoughts down quickly enough.

Motivating forces

There is no particular emphasis on one part of the writing over another. Everything works well together, showing a good balance between the various parts of Galileo's personality. The rightward trend and narrower right margin reveal his forward thinking nature and desire to make an important contribution to the world.

Between the lines

Some of the baselines in Galileo's writing are concave. A baseline that tends to dip in the middle in this way, then climbs back up toward the end is made by someone who starts out on new projects rather slowly. The writer may complain that there is too much to do, or that he or she has to do everything with no help from others. As the writer gets further along, however, enthusiasm grows and the negative outlook is overcome. He or she will make a strong finish to the project.

Adì 7 di Gennaio 1610 Giove si vedeva col Cannone
3 stelle fisse così ✳ ⊕ ✳ delle quali se ne il cur
minor si vedeva. à dì 8 appariva così ⊕ ✳ ✳ ✳ era d
diretto et nõ retrogrado come dicono i calculatori.
Adì 9 in nugolo. à dì 10 si vedeva con ———— ✳ ✳ ⊕ ciò
giuto la più occidentale si che à recita quãto si può credere.
Adì 11 era in questa guisa ✳ ✳ ⊕ et la stella più vic
à Giove era la metà minore dell'altra, et vicinissima all'a
dove che le altre sere erano le dette stelle apparite tutte
di egual grandezza et tra di loro equalmente lontane; dal che
appare intorno à Giove esser 3 altre stelle erranti invisibili
ogn'uno sino à questo tempo.
Adì 12 si vedde in tale costituzione ✳ ⊕ ✳ era la stel
occidentale poco minor della orientale, et giove era in mezzo lontane
da l'una et da l'altra quanto il suo diametro è circa: et forse er
una terza vicinissima et vicinissima à ♃ verso oriente; anzi pur in e
veramente havendo io più diligenza osservato, et hebbe più imbrunita
notti.
Adì 13 havendo benissimo fermato lo strumento si veddero vicinissime à ♃
4 stelle in questa costituzione ✳ ⊕ ✳ ✳ è meglio così ✳ ⊕ ✳
e tutte apparivano della medesima grandezza, lo spazio delle 3 occid
nõ era maggiore del diametro di ♃ . et erano fra di loro notab
più vicine che le altre sere; ne erano in linea retta esquisitamente
avanti ma è media delle 3 occidentali era un poco elevata, o vero
più occidentale alquanto depressa; sono queste stelle tutte molto lucide
piccolissime et altre fisse et apparivano della medesima grandezza nõ
così splendenti.
Adì 14 fù nugolo. Adì 15 era così ⊕ ✳ ✳ ✳ ✳ la prossima
♃ era la minore et le altre di mano in mano maggiori: gl'interstitii
tra ♃ et le 3 seguenti erano, quãto il diametro di ♃ ma la 4ª era

♃.
♃ long. 71.38 Lat. 1.13   Me: 2.30 una iteramente linea retta, ma come mostra
                           1.13   l'esempio, erano al solito lucidissime ne che
                           1.17   lo, et niente scintillavano ...

Sketches of Jupiter

This page from Galileo's own notebook shows his notes and sketches on his observation of Jupiter. Galileo discovered the four largest satellites circling Jupiter. Among his other astronomical discoveries were the craters of the moon, sunspots, and the phases of Venus. He also correctly deduced that the Milky Way was made up of many distant stars. His astronomical observations led him to believe that the earth revolved around the sun, an idea that he was forced to recant by the Roman Catholic church, which had him placed under house arrest for the last eight years of his life.

Ulysses S. Grant

18TH U.S. PRESIDENT (1822–1885)

Ulysses Grant, the son of a tanner, was born in Ohio. He graduated only in the middle of his class at West Point and was later unsuccessful in numerous business ventures. Grant was an outstanding Union general during the American Civil War, and was elected to the presidency in 1869, serving two terms. Upon learning he had throat cancer, he became concerned about being able to provide for his family. He decided to write his memoirs, which earned nearly $450,000, and died shortly after their completion.

Personality overview

Grant's handwriting emphasizes movement. The rapid speed can be seen in the thready form, narrow margins, and strong right slant in the upper zone. He responded with gut reactions and had a tendency to rush headlong into things. As a result it is likely that he would often make a quick decision, then, once committed, realize he had undertaken a task that he really did not want to do. On the positive side, Grant could throw himself into a cause he believed in and, with that dynamic upper zone, was able to work tirelessly to support it.

Relationships

The intensity of the slant reflects someone in desperate need of affection. However, the wide spaces and undeveloped middle zone show that it was hard for him to accept such affection. Nonetheless, Grant's emotions were easily touched, making life a series of highs and lows. The flattened middle zone reflects the need to defend a fragile ego, which is where much of his energy was spent. To that end he could be manipulative, this being another function of the thready form. Although the lower zone is proportionate in length, it is rather narrow showing insecurity and fear of change. He probably judged his own performance and found it lacking.

Intellectual forces

Grant's intelligence is evident in the well-organized arrangement of space on the page. The problem was that in thinking so fast he had to discard information that did not further his views. Thus, he might simply scratch the surface of a subject when in reality there was much more to be gleaned. The retraced and narrow upper-zone letters demonstrate a mind mostly closed to new ideas, so he would be more likely to repeat his mistakes than to learn from them.

Physical drives

The writing has a tremendous amount of movement, but without much force. The pressure appears light and the middle zone is so thready as to appear "strung out." This strung-out quality gives a good indication of the level of stress that Grant was under at the time of writing. This is hardly surprising given that he was writing in the midst of war.

Motivating forces

The greatest saving grace in this script is the spatial arrangement. Grant's ability to see the big picture and to take into account the various factors at work would cover a multitude of other problems and flaws.

Between the lines

Although no single letter should be considered outside the context of the writing, some graphologists assign meanings to particular letters. One of these is the lower case *k*—when there is a large buckle, it indicates rebelliousness; when looped around the stem, it shows affection; slashing bars through the stem show aggression; bars that do not touch the stem, as is the case with some of Grant's *k*'s, show aloofness.

A letter written by Ulysses Grant to Jones, December 26 1864

Jones is most likely J. Russell Jones, Grant's old friend, by then a Chicago businessman.

> ... during the war. Heretofore when they have met disaster they had the material still left back to recruit their Armies. Now the loss of a thousand men cannot be replaced unless they resort to the darkey. Him they are afraid of and will not use him unless as a last desperate resort.
> ... are all flourishing.
> Respectfully yours,
> U.S. Grant

John Hancock

REVOLUTIONARY LEADER (1737–1793)

John Hancock was born in Massachusetts. He graduated from Harvard and went to work for a wealthy uncle. Active in the politics of his day, he served as a selectman and member of the Massachusetts General Court, and, later, as president of the Continental Congress. His birthday is celebrated as National Handwriting Day, thanks to his bold signature on the Declaration of Independence, which he is said to have deliberately made that way so King George could read it without his spectacles. Hancock was elected governor of Massachusetts in 1780.

Personality overview

The emphasis is on form, or the way the writing looks. As he intended it to, Hancock's signature stands out with its large capitals, overall large size, and ornate paraph (the flourish at the end of a signature) underneath. In addition, the handwriting in the text is elaborate, with unnecessary details added to the basic script. For instance, the final *d* in many words turns back to the left in a large loop and arcs back over the word. A form-conscious handwriting is adopted by one who likes to draw attention to him- or herself and make a big impression. Whether there is substance to back up the first impression is entirely another question.

Relationships

Another aspect of form consciousness is that the writer maintains a facade and is afraid to let anyone see what is underneath. Consequently, although he was a people-oriented person, Hancock's basic attitude was one of reserve and conservatism. He tended to bottle up his feelings and kept them to himself. He could not allow himself to be spontaneous, lest some undesirable part of himself accidentally be seen. This characteristic is evident in the arcade letter forms and slow writing speed.

Intellectual forces

The showiness of the writing, especially the final strokes that go into the upper zone where they do not belong, suggests someone who was in love with his own rhetoric. Hancock had a flair for the dramatic and when he had something to say, it was never simple but an epic story. His thinking style was systematic and left no room for intuition, which he ignored in favor of logic.

Physical drives

The lower zone is extremely long and thin and this is in conflict with the overall slow, picturesque style of the rest of the writing sample. Hancock felt restless and needed to be doing something physical all the time. It is difficult for this type of writer to relax and he was no doubt irritated by inactivity.

Motivating forces

The arcade style of writing and steady return to the baseline indicate that for Hancock a major motivating factor was his need for security. The baseline represents the ground on which one stands, so for him it was important to feel that his feet were planted firmly on the ground and his material needs were properly cared for.

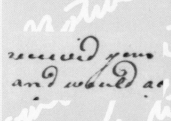

Between the lines

Elaboration in handwriting refers to extra strokes and flourishes added to the basic copybook model. These must be attractive and not detract from legibility if they are to be considered in a positive light. When harmonious, such elaboration signifies fullness of feeling and imagination. However, an overly embellished writing style reflects a waste of time—both the writer's and the reader's. Hancock's script, while not too elaborate for the time, would be considered time wasting today.

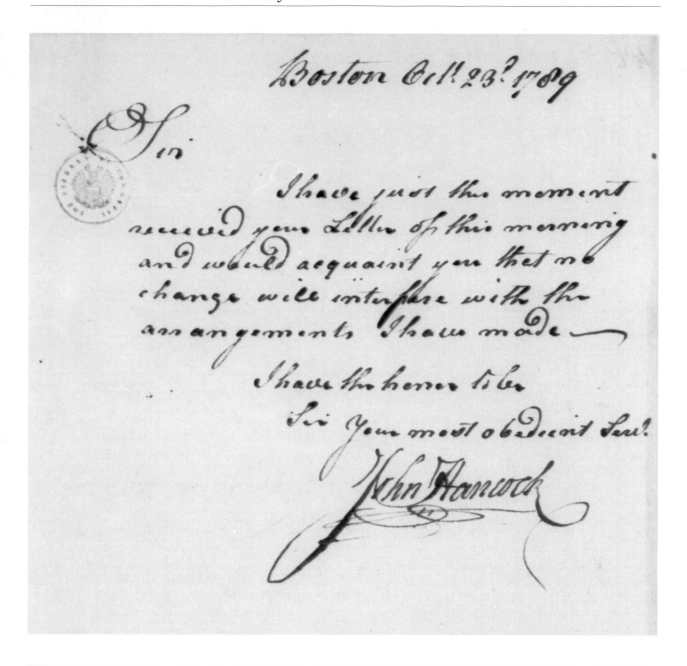

A letter written by John Hancock

Boston Oct 23rd 1789

Sir

I have just this moment received your Letter of this morning and would acquaint you that no change will interfere with the arrangements I have made.
I have the honor to be Sir your most obedient Servt.

John Hancock

Ernest Hemingway

PULITZER PRIZE-WINNING WRITER (1899–1961)

Ernest Hemingway began writing in high school and later went to work as a foreign news correspondent, often covering war stories. His first important book, *Our Time*, was published in 1925, and the following year he found success with *The Sun Also Rises*. In 1953, he received the Pulitzer Prize in fiction for *The Old Man and the Sea*, although his most popular novel is probably *A Farewell to Arms*. Hemingway led an adventurous life and married four times. However, he also suffered a history of depression and eventually killed himself.

Personality overview

Hemingway's writing has the loose, arrhythmic style and falling baselines often seen in people suffering depression. Although tremendous energy is present in some wide and long lower loops, he was clearly very down at the time of writing. The soft letter forms represent an emotional nature, mitigated by the upright slant and wide spaces.

Relationships

There is no artifice in these simplified forms and Hemingway was willing to be seen for who he was. The long, firm downstrokes in the lower zone, meanwhile, indicate persistence and determination. He also required plenty of space in which to work, so would not have appreciated interruption. The rounded downstroke on his personal pronoun, *I*, reveals an emotionally dependent person who, with the wide picture of space, was not always able to ask for what he needed from others.

Intellectual forces

The broad upper-zone loops and long, strong *t*-crosses validate his imagination and ability to make his proliferation of ideas work. The page is generally well organized, despite the falling baselines, so Hemingway understood where things belonged in his life. His letter forms are simple, with no embellishments to take away from the basic meaning of the points he wanted to make.

Physical drives

A hearty appetite for action and adventure is clear in the long, well-pressured lower-zone downstrokes and some wide lower loops. The same extra-long downstrokes also suggest restlessness, a need for freedom. Additionally, several *t*-crosses fall short of the stem, so Hemingway probably had trouble committing to a specific, long-term course of action, just in case something more interesting came along.

Motivating forces

The basic conflict in Hemingway's handwriting is seen in the signs of creativity (original forms, wide upper loops, heavy *t*-crosses) versus the inhibiting forces of wide word spacing and upright slant. Even though he was highly productive, he may have felt pulled in different directions, and so was left with a pessimistic outlook on life.

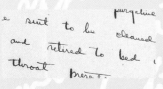

Between the lines

The direction in which letters slant plays a part in demonstrating the writer's emotional responses. One whose writing slants to the right leans toward others and is generally warmhearted. A leftward slant moves away from others and the writer does not want to be known. Upright writing such as Hemingway's signifies a coolheaded, objective person who does not get carried away by his or her emotions.

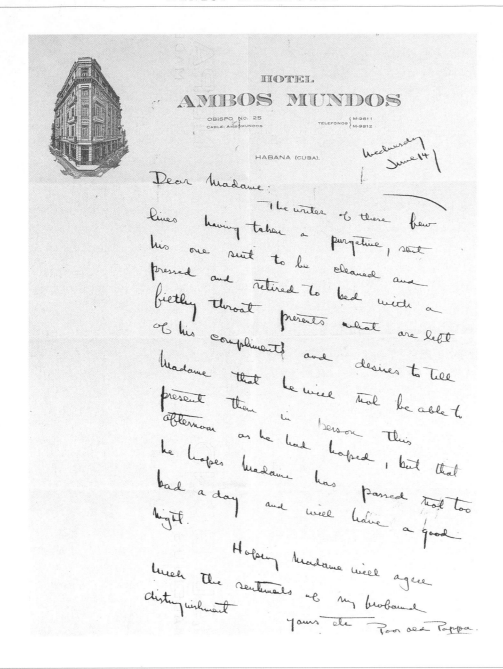

A letter written to Jane Mason at the British-American Clinic in Havana, 14 June 1933

In early June, Jane had either jumped or fallen from a low balcony and a few days earlier had escaped serious injury in a car accident.

Dear Madame

The writer of these few lines having taken purgative, sent his one suit to be cleaned and pressed and retired to bed with a filthy throat presents what are left of his compliments and desires to tell Madame that he will not be able to present them in person this afternoon as he had hoped, but that he hopes Madame has not passed too bad a day and will have a good night.

Hoping Madame will agree with the sentiments of my distinguishment

Yours etc Poor Old Pappa

Jimi Hendrix

American Rock Guitarist (1942–1970)

Jimi Hendrix, born in Seattle, Washington State, was one of the most influential musicians in rock history. A self-taught guitarist, he began playing to audiences while serving in the American military, and later played in bands with such artists as the Isley Brothers, Little Richard, and Sam Cooke. He became famous in England when he and his band, The Jimi Hendrix Experience, had a top 10 hit with their first single, "Hey Joe." With his wild hairstyle and bright costumes, Hendrix's unique sound and style enthralled audiences before his untimely death, the result of an overdose.

Personality overview

Jimi Hendrix's handwriting is filled with feelings. The loops and swirls reveal a dramatic person tossed this way and that on a sea of emotion. The large, rounded forms clearly demonstrate a need to be in the thick of things, the life and soul of every party. The pressure is sporadic, however, with the heaviest strokes on the horizontal plane, that is in the *t*-crosses and long dashes that substitute for punctuation. This demonstrates how Hendrix's energy came in fits and starts and was quickly depleted. He would completely throw himself into whatever it was he was doing then, when it was over, be totally drained.

Relationships

A personal relationship with Hendrix would not have been for the faint of heart. The strong variability in the writing reveals his theatrical, unpredictable style, and anyone close to him would have been in for a wild and turbulent emotional ride. The twists and turns in an often incomplete lower zone reveal past painful experiences that left their mark on his sexual attitudes. This may well have made it difficult for him to form truly intimate connections with other people.

Intellectual forces

Hendrix's original style and simplified forms reveal a resourceful person who would not accept things just because they were traditionally done in a particular way. The horizontal movement on the *t*-bars indicates strong intellectual drive. Bright and intensely creative, Hendrix made things happen the way he wanted them. The increasing size of letters at the ends of words show his insistence, literally, on having the last word.

Physical drives

The bouncy rhythm and emphasis on movement are hallmarks of one who needed to be constantly active and on the go. Forced to sit quietly for any length of time, Hendrix would have become bored and restless. Some part of his body always had to be moving.

Motivating forces

The original, stylish capitals of the sample are mostly large and well-formed, showing pride in his achievements and an ability to project a confidence that, deep down, he may have not always felt. The weak *J* in the signature suggests uncertainty, although it is larger than the rest of his name.

Between the lines

Pressure in handwriting, which in Hendrix's case is quite sporadic, reveals a person's basic life force. There should be a natural ebb and flow of this energy, with an emphasis on the downstroke (coming back to self) and lighter pressure on the upstroke (releasing away from self). When this pattern is reversed, it suggests a writer who interrupts the natural flow and makes life more difficult by continually pushing. The heavier the overall pressure, the longer the writer's memory of emotional events.

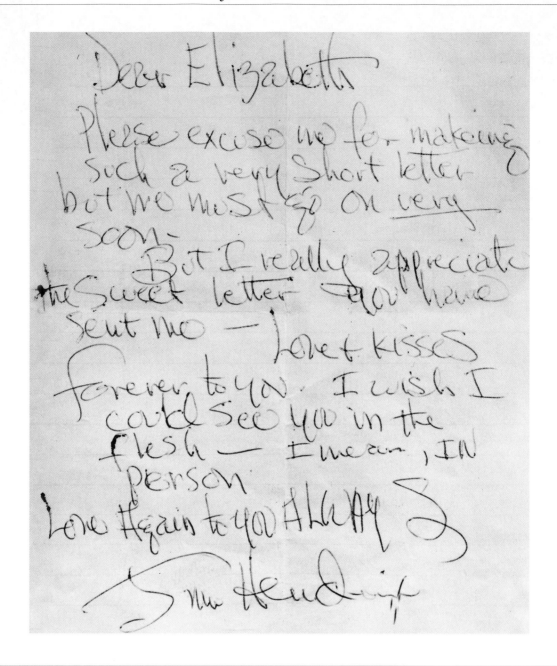

A letter to a fan written by Hendrix in 1967 prior to a performance

Dear Elizabeth

Please excuse me for making such a very short letter but we must go on very soon.
But I really appreciate the sweet letter you have sent me—
Love and kisses forever to you. I wish I could see you in the flesh—I mean in person
Love again to you always

Jimi Hendrix

Henry VIII

BRITISH MONARCH (1491–1547)

Henry VIII was born in Greenwich and ascended to the throne at the age of 18. A talented ruler, he is probably best known for having a total of six wives—two of whom he later executed for alleged treason—and for breaking away from the Roman Catholic church when it would not grant him a divorce from his first wife, Catherine of Aragon. An athlete, poet and musician, Henry desperately wanted a son and heir. However, his only son, Edward, was frail and it was his two daughters, the princesses Mary and Elizabeth, who both later ruled in their own right.

Personality overview

Henry's handwriting emphasizes vigorous movement with its moderately large overall size in a tight, compact picture of space, the mark of a busy person who crowded as many activities into each day as possible. There is a certain capricious quality to the changeable slant, size, and baseline. While weakness is not inferred, inasmuch as he would not allow himself to be pushed around, the evidence indicates that Henry would certainly have changed his mind if and when presented with more attractive possibilities.

Relationships

The heavy pressure and forcefulness in the writing suggest someone with the sexual and physical appetites for which Henry was famous. This was the type of person who needed to be adored and had to surround himself with many admirers. Otherwise, considering the close word spacing and the large size, he would feel at a loose end if left to his own devices for very long.

Intellectual forces

There is a greater emphasis on doing than on thinking. This in no way suggests a lack of intelligence, but simply a focus on the more pragmatic, down-to-earth realities of daily life. In fact, the writing speed demonstrates a rapid thinker who could turn his attention to several tasks simultaneously.

Physical drives

The blotchy, muddy quality cannot be explained simply by the writing instruments of the day, as most of the writing has at least moderate clarity. Instead, it reveals the uninhibited indulgence of the writer's baser urges. These included Henry's need for food, sex, money, and material pursuits. There is also a restlessness in the script, with the writing movement going in every direction. Henry clearly needed to be on the go and involved in a variety of physical activities for much of the time. There are some sharp, heavy strokes going into the lower zone, which attest to a cruel streak.

Motivating forces

With the writing so crowded and the signature so large, it can be deduced that Henry did not allow himself enough room to create a clear perspective on his life. Unable to step back and look at the big picture, he put his own needs and desires first. Freud might have called this an "id writing," since for Henry fulfilling his own basic drives were his uppermost concern.

Between the lines

In handwriting analysis the small letters show the writer's real self, while the capital letters show the ideal self. Capitals that are about two to three times the size of the middle-zone height reveal a healthy ego and self-image. Much larger, ornate capitals, as in Henry VIII's writing, are made by those who wish to draw attention to themselves. Much smaller capitals are a sign of modesty or shyness.

Undated letter by Henry VIII

Myne awne good cardinall I recomende me unto you as hastely as … so it is that by … is … tedius and paynefull therfor the most part off this … I have comyttyd to our trusty … thys berrar to be declared to you by … to … we wolde you shyulde geff credens nevertheless to thys that folowith. I thought nott but to make hym … nor non other but you and I … is that I wolde you … make good … on the duke of suffolk on the duke off bukyngam on my lord off north homberland on my lord off darby on my lord off… and on other… you thynke proper to see what they do on this… no more to you at thys tyme but … the hand off your loving master henry.

Adolf Hitler

GERMAN DICTATOR (1889–1945)

In his youth Adolf Hitler wanted to become an artist, but twice failed the entrance examination to the Academy in his home country of Austria. Decorated for bravery in World War I, he quickly became leader of the Nazi Party in the chaos of postwar Germany. Coming to power by a combination of guile, nationalism, intimidation, and luck, he was appointed chancellor of Germany on January 30, 1933. In 1939 he invaded Poland, which began World War II. Responsible for the deaths of more than 12 million people during the war, Hitler committed suicide on his impending defeat April 30, 1945.

Personality overview

A cruel, angry man is clearly evident in the combination of angles and thread connective forms. Add to these the muddy pressure and all the hallmarks of an inharmonious personality with an authoritarian attitude and lack of tolerance can be seen. Writers with such a high degree of angles tend to be judgmental and see everything in terms of black or white to the point of pathology. For them there is no in-between. The signature and several lines point downward, a sign of depression and discouragement. There was little or no sense of humor to relieve Hitler's evident irritability.

Relationships

The capital letters are tall, showing Hitler's pride in his achievements. However, his inflexibility is the strongest characteristic and no doubt made him a very difficult person to be around. Because he always had to be right and his temper was so explosive, as seen in the heavy *i*-dots and horizontal strokes in the upper zone, one would have to walk on eggshells all the time. Except for some minor threadiness, the sharply pointed angles are unrelieved. Hitler could be quite charming on those occasions when it suited him. The letters are also narrow, indicating personal shyness or inhibition.

Intellectual forces

The linear quality of the writing shows a strong intellectual bent. However, the upper zone is not particularly developed, suggesting Hitler was satisfied with his current philosophy and not interested in exploring anything new or different that might contradict his beliefs. A personality type who would actively seek out controversy, he could become extremely argumentative in promoting his point of view.

Physical drives

The emphasis is on action and movement. The strong pressure and horizontal expansion show that Hitler had a great deal of stamina and endurance. In fact, his energy probably seemed boundless to those around him. The writing moves so fast and is so strongly slanted to the right that it is like a runaway train, impulsive and often reckless in making decisions and carrying them out.

Motivating forces

A man of excessively strong opinions, seen in the sharp points, Hitler's motivation was to promote his own viewpoint at the expense of everyone else's. While this is not news to anyone who has read history, perhaps the fact that Hitler's handwriting so clearly shows his intent is.

Between the lines

Mud in handwriting pertains to a quality of the stroke. Pastose writing has thick strokes made without pressure, whereas muddy handwriting is thick and blotchy because of an excessive of pressure on the pen nib. Such muddy handwriting may be a sign of ill health or—as was probably the case with Hitler—of one whose baser drives have been allowed to run wild in an excess of sex, drugs, or alcohol.

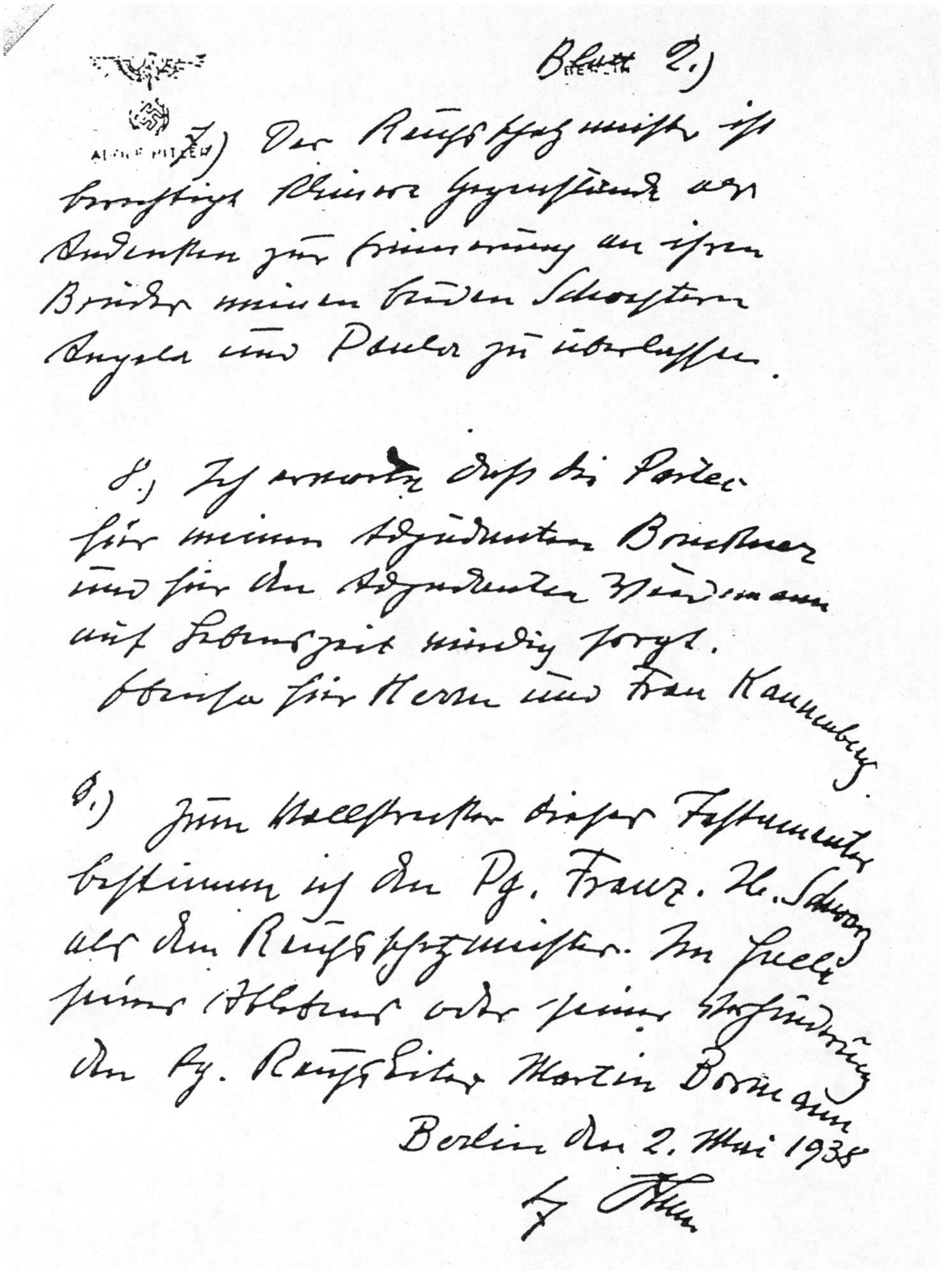

ADOLF HITLER

Blatt 2.)

7.) Der Reichsschatzmeister ist berechtigt kleinere Gegenstände als Andenken zur Erinnerung an ihren Bruder meinen beiden Schwestern Angela und Paula zu überlassen.

8.) Ich erwarte daß die Partei für meinen Adjudanten Brückner und für den Adjudanten Wiedemann auf Lebenszeit würdig sorgt. Ebenso für Herrn und Frau Kannenberg.

9.) Zum Vollstrecker dieses Testamentes bestimme ich den Pg. Franz. X. Schwarz als den Reichsschatzmeister. Im Falle seines Ablebens oder seiner Verhinderung den Pg. Reichsleiter Martin Bormann

Berlin den 2. Mai 1938

A. Hitler

An early draft of Hitler's will, May 2, 1938

7) The Party Treasurer is entitled to hand over smaller objects to my sisters Angela and Paula as keepsakes.
8) It is my wish that the Party make generous provision for my adjutants Brückner and Weidemann throughout their lives, and also for Herr and Frau Kannenberg.
9) I appoint Party Comrade Franz X Schwarz, the Party Treasurer, as my executor. In the case of his death or any other impediment, I appoint Party Comrade and Reichs-Führer Martin Bormann in his stead.
Berlin, 2 May, 1938
Adolf Hitler

Thomas Jefferson

THIRD U.S. PRESIDENT (1743–1826)

Thomas Jefferson is perhaps best known as the principal author of the Declaration of Independence, but was also an important political leader and a learned philosopher. Prior to entering politics Jefferson was a wealthy planter in Virginia, but went on to become a great champion of freedom whose public career spanned four decades. This included two terms as president of the United States. After his retirement Jefferson founded the University of Virginia, and his vast collection of classical texts formed the basis for the Library of Congress.

Personality overview

Jefferson's handwriting has a strong sense of direction in one who would not give up. A prolific communicator, he covered the page with his words, suggesting a cautious approach to spending time and money. This is not to imply stinginess—the letters themselves are well-rounded and not squeezed together, as would be expected in a parsimonious person. Rather, he was a careful planner who made sure his needs would not outlast his resources.

Relationships

The i-dots are close to the stems, showing loyalty to a person or an idea. The words are written close together with a moderate right slant, reflecting a person who cared deeply about others but who did not get carried away with his empathy. The high degree of connected-ness shows one who found it easy to make contacts and cared that his listener understood him. In fact, some might have considered him argumentative when he would not let go of an idea until they capitulated.

Intellectual forces

While the connected writing indicates a logical thinker who built one idea upon another, Jefferson also used simplified combinations, such as the connection from o to f in of. This shows the ability to understand a concept rapidly and move on to the next thought. He was a deductive, albeit a generally conventional, thinker with an orientation toward the fine details.

Physical drives

It may have taken Jefferson some time to warm up, as seen in the medium speed of the writing, but once he got going the amount of output alone suggests strong drive and stamina. In addition, the overall writing size is small, with a very steady rhythm, showing that he had the capacity to accomplish a great deal by planning and then acting on that plan. The short lower zone suggests that he knew his limitations and stuck within them.

Motivating forces

The chief connective form in this writing is the arcade. In combination with highly connected letters in a compact but not overcrowded script, this indicates one who worked hard to make sure the needs of those who depended on him were well catered for. Jefferson would have been ashamed to be seen as less than totally responsible, so was motivated by the need to create a secure environment.

Between the lines

The invisible line that a person writes on, called the baseline, symbolizes how that person approaches their goals. A line so straight that it seems written on a ruler is indicative of someone who leaves no room to adapt to the exigencies of a particular situation. On the other hand, if the baseline moves up and down a lot, this shows that the writer is constantly distracted from his or her goals. Jefferson's baseline is straight but shows a small degree of variability, which is desirable.

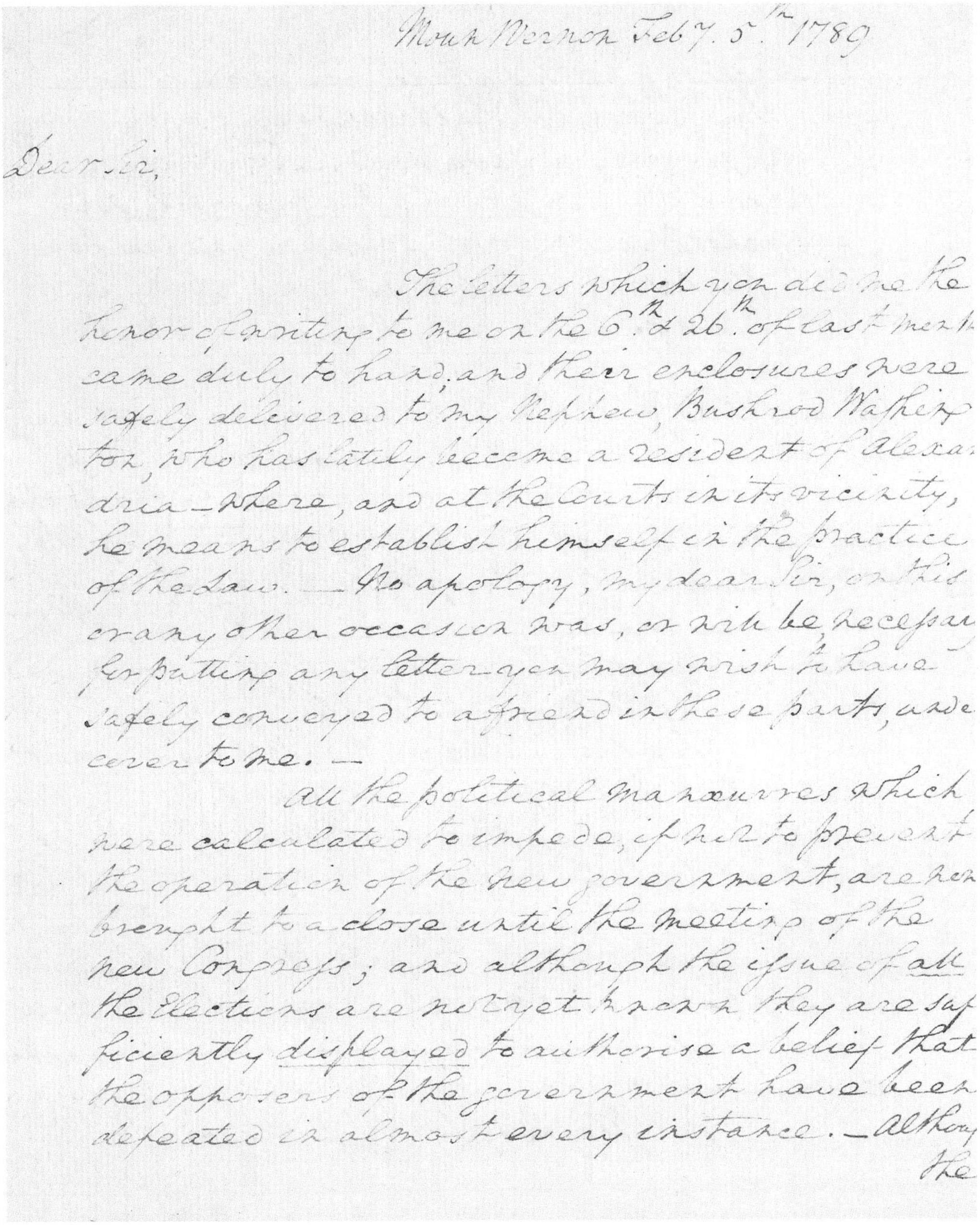

Mount Vernon Feby. 5th 1789

Dear Sir,

The letters which you did me the honor of writing to me on the 6th & 26th of last month came duly to hand, and their enclosures were safely delivered to my Nephew, Bushrod Washington, who has lately become a resident of Alexandria—where, and at the courts in its vicinity, he means to establish himself in the practice of the Law. — No apology, my dear Sir, on this or any other occasion was, or will be necessary for putting any letter you may wish to have safely conveyed to a friend in these parts, under cover to me. —

All the political manoeuvres which were calculated to impede, if not to prevent the operation of the new government, are now brought to a close until the meeting of the new Congress; and although the issue of all the Elections are not yet known they are sufficiently displayed to authorise a belief that the opposers of the government have been defeated in almost every instance. — Although the

Part of a letter from Jefferson to George Washington

... Feb 5th 1789

Dear Sir

The letters which you did me the honor of writing to me on the 6th & 26th of last month came duly to hand and their enclosures were safely delivered to my nephew ... who has lately become a resident of Alexandria—where, and at the courts in its vicinity, he means to establish himself in the practice of the law.—No apology, my dear Sir, on this or any other occasion was, or will be necessary for putting any letter you may wish to have safely conveyed to a friend in these parts, under cover to me.

All the political manoeuvres which were calculated to impede, if not to prevent the operation of the new government, are now brought to a close until the meeting of the new Congress; and although the issue of <u>all</u> the elections are not yet known they are sufficiently <u>displayed</u> to authorize a belief that the opposers of the government have been defeated in almost every instance.—Although the...

Jacqueline Kennedy Onassis

AMERICAN FIRST LADY (1929–1994)

Jacqueline Kennedy Onassis was born into the socially prominent Bouvier family and after attending university worked as a columnist and photographer. In 1953 she married the man who was to become the 35th U.S. president. She and John F. Kennedy had five children, but only two survived. A stylish trendsetter, Jacqueline Kennedy set up a fine arts commission in the White House. In 1968, five years after her husband was assassinated, she married Aristotle Onassis, one of the richest men in the world. The marriage was to last until his death in 1975.

Personality overview

The two samples, one before and one after John F. Kennedy's death, starkly illustrate how handwriting can change after a traumatic event. While the general style is still the same (her basic personality did not alter), the second writing is much more compressed, showing Jacqueline's withdrawal from society. The writing style is sophisticated, revealing her flair and style, with diagonal strokes flying into the upper zone, the area of aspirations and ideals. In the first sample especially, she was looking at the future with optimism and ambition.

Relationships

The upright slant and simplified forms indicate someone who did not easily involve herself in social relationships. She had great charm and the ability to express herself well, as seen in the threadiness and interesting connections in the upper zone, but the narrow letters and spare lower zone forms are evidence of selectivity when it came to choosing friends. She often made the first letter of a word larger, a sign of someone who outwardly displayed more confidence than she might have felt.

Intellectual forces

The writing is simplified to the essentials, and the letter forms are original. Along with the emphasis on the upper zone, this paints a picture of an intellectually oriented person. Mrs. Onassis's interest in exploring new areas prompted her to seek continuing mental stimulation, without which she would have soon become bored.

Physical drives

The earlier writing has a much greater level of activity, although the focus is more on mental than physical goals. The second sample, with its contracted movement, implies a pulling in of energy, an act of self-protection. In this the middle zone becomes even more deemphasized, showing an avoidance of dealing with day-to-day routine and relationships in favor of intellectual pursuits.

Motivating forces

The need to create something new is the chief motivating factor, although in the later sample Mrs. Onassis turned more to self-exploration. The signature, with its large capitals, reveals a focus more on the ideal than the real self.

Between the lines

In handwriting, the overall pictorial quality is called the form level, or Formniveau. High form level, as in Mrs. Onassis's case, means the writing looks well organized and balanced, suggesting a well-integrated personality. Low form level means a disorganized, unbalanced page. This denotes a lack of integration in some area of the personality, depending on where the imbalance exists: in space, form, or movement.

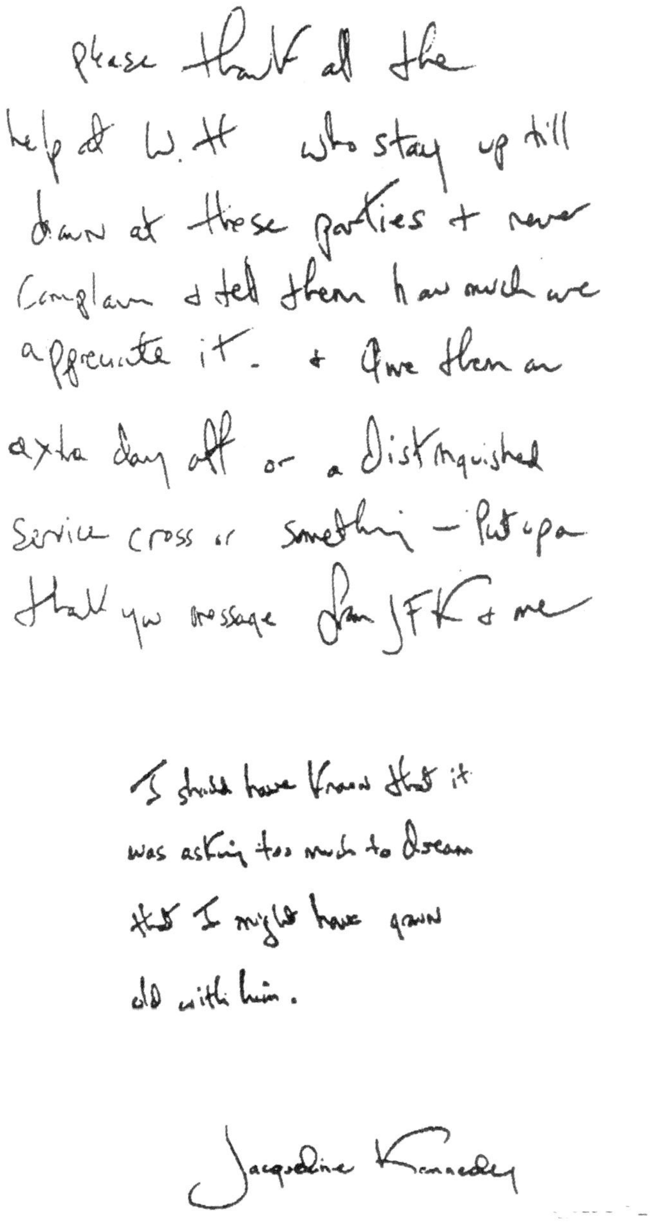

Please thank all the help at W.H. who stay up till dawn at these parties & never complain & tell them how much we appreciate it. & give them an extra day off or a distinguished service cross or something—Put up a thank you message from JFK and me

I should have known that it was asking too much to dream that I might have grown old with him.

Jacqueline Kennedy

Notes written by Jacqueline Kennedy, before and after John F. Kennedy's assassination

Please thank all the help at W.H. who stay up till dawn at these parties & never complain & tell them how much we appreciate it. & give them an extra day off or a distinguished service cross or something—Put up a thank you message from JFK and me

I should have known that it was asking too much to dream that I might have grown old with him.

Jacqueline Kennedy

John F. Kennedy

35TH U.S. PRESIDENT (1917–1963)

John Fitzgerald Kennedy was the youngest man, and the first Catholic, to be elected president of the United States. After graduating from Harvard, he distinguished himself as a hero in World War II and later went on to become a Democratic congressman and senator. Then, in 1960, Kennedy beat Richard Nixon to become president. During his short term in office he advanced the cause of civil rights and, despite facing a number of foreign crises, including the Cuba missile crisis, managed to avert nuclear war with the Soviet Union in 1962. Kennedy was assassinated in Dallas on November 22, 1963.

Personality overview

Kennedy's handwriting has the dynamism of a visionary and an executive. He was undoubtedly an ideas person who could look ahead and visualize the future. While the *t*-bars fly into the stratosphere of the upper zone, they remain connected to the stem, so he was also able to stay in touch with reality. The writing has narrow letters with wide spaces in between, reflecting a basically shy person who had learned to behave in an outgoing manner when appropriate.

Relationships

The long lower zone dwarfs the middle zone, indicating strong physical drives. Add the pastose strokes, and this becomes a sign of restlessness in one who used sexual activity more as a tranquilizer than as a means to get emotionally close to his partner. The strong right slant indicates a responsive, compassionate person but it also shows that Kennedy would chafe when forced to wait. However, the threadiness is evidence that he could temper this impatience with charm.

Intellectual forces

The writing is simplified with wide spacing, evidence that Kennedy was able to see the big picture. In fact, he was not particularly detail oriented, as seen in some missing *i*-dots and the high degree of threaded letter forms. To get things done he would have needed someone to follow behind his many lofty ideas and implement them, handling the administrative details— otherwise, they would not have gotten off the ground.

Physical drives

The strongest aspect of Kennedy's handwriting is the picture of movement, which reveals a vigorous, active person who could not sit still for very long at a time. It is likely that some part of his body had to be in motion all the time—it would not be surprising, even if he was sitting calmly behind a desk, to look underneath and see him impatiently tapping his toes.

Motivating forces

The emphasis in Kennedy's handwriting is on simplified movement in a picture of wide spacing, which means that his motivating force was the driving need to make improvements in the world around him. It would have been impossible for him to just sit back and do things the way they had always been done. Kennedy's ability to look ahead and anticipate the future also put him on the cutting edge.

Between the lines

The amount of space between letters reveals the writer's sense of internal freedom, the standard width of that space being the width of a letter *n* in the writer's script. With an adequate amount of space, the writer is spontaneous and outgoing, while narrow letter spacing signifies impulsive behavior. With a good middle-zone width, extra-wide spaces such as in Kennedy's writing reveal a talkative, expansive person.

for your country — my fellow
citizen of the world — ask not
or others
what America will do for you —
give for
but rather what you can do
for freedom   Rather ask of us —
the same high standard of
sacrifice and strength of heart
and will that we need from
you.   Its alliance for
war + progress will to for great

Excerpt from John F. Kennedy's inaugural speech

... for your country—my fellow citizens of the world—ask not what America (or others) will do for you—but rather what you (give for) can do for freedom. Rather ask of us—the same high standard of sacrifice and strength of heart and will that we need from you...

Robert E. Lee

CONFEDERATE GENERAL (1807–1870)

Robert E. Lee was the fourth child of a genteel but impoverished Virginia family that boasted several famous figures, including his father, "Light-Horse Harry" Lee, a calvary leader in the Revolutionary War. Lee attended the United States Military Academy at West Point, where his natural talents and gifts blossomed and he graduated second in his class. He went on to become what was considered to be the most successful commander of all the Southern armies during the American Civil War. His decision to surrender at Appomattox Court House famously ended the war in 1865.

Personality overview

Lee's handwriting has a strong linear appearance and a pressure pattern that shows the straight downstrokes to be quite heavy. The significance of this is that, while others might crumble in the face of opposition, Lee had the fortitude to stand firm in his decisions. The sheer force of his will would have kept him from caving in. At the same time, the writing is softened by connective garland forms and a right slant, these revealing a basically empathetic nature.

Relationships

The garlands and angle pattern reveal Lee's preference for maintaining equilibrium and for building a consensus whenever possible. However, when his values or principles were called into question you could expect him to come up with a sharp response. The tall, narrow upper zone and clean strokes reveal a highly principled individual with a strong appreciation for right and wrong. Lee was a person who stood firmly by his beliefs and stayed loyal to his philosophies. With his mild-mannered demeanor, he might have seemed to lack strong emotions, but the right slant in a retraced upper zone suggests that he was simply not comfortable with expressing them openly.

Intellectual forces

If an idea was not firmly based on logic and grounded in common sense, Lee would not accept it. The v-shapes in the middle zone reflect an investigative mind that would not trust in gut reactions. Rather, he would insist on facts and figures before he was convinced. His habit of thinking sequentially rather than holistically, as seen in the strong connectedness, might have caused him to miss some of the more subtle nuances of a problem.

Physical drives

The regularity in the writing, combined with angles and retracing, reveals a great deal of pent-up energy. The same characteristics denote firm determination and an unwavering strength of purpose. At the same time, horizontal movement is missing in the upper zone, and the right margin drifts to the left, reflecting Lee's concern for what might be coming up in the future.

Motivating forces

Tall capital letters and a clear signature reveal a sense of pride in his achievements, and this was undoubtedly a motivating factor for Lee. He was impelled to live up to his own standards to prove his own worth, perhaps because his father died when he was a child.

Between the lines

Handwriting is made up of two basic types of strokes: straight lines and curved lines. Every letter is made up of one or a combination of both types of stroke, but many writers use a preponderance of one or the other. Those who choose a rounded, curvy style have an emotional approach, while those, such as Lee, who prefer a linear style are more intellectually oriented.

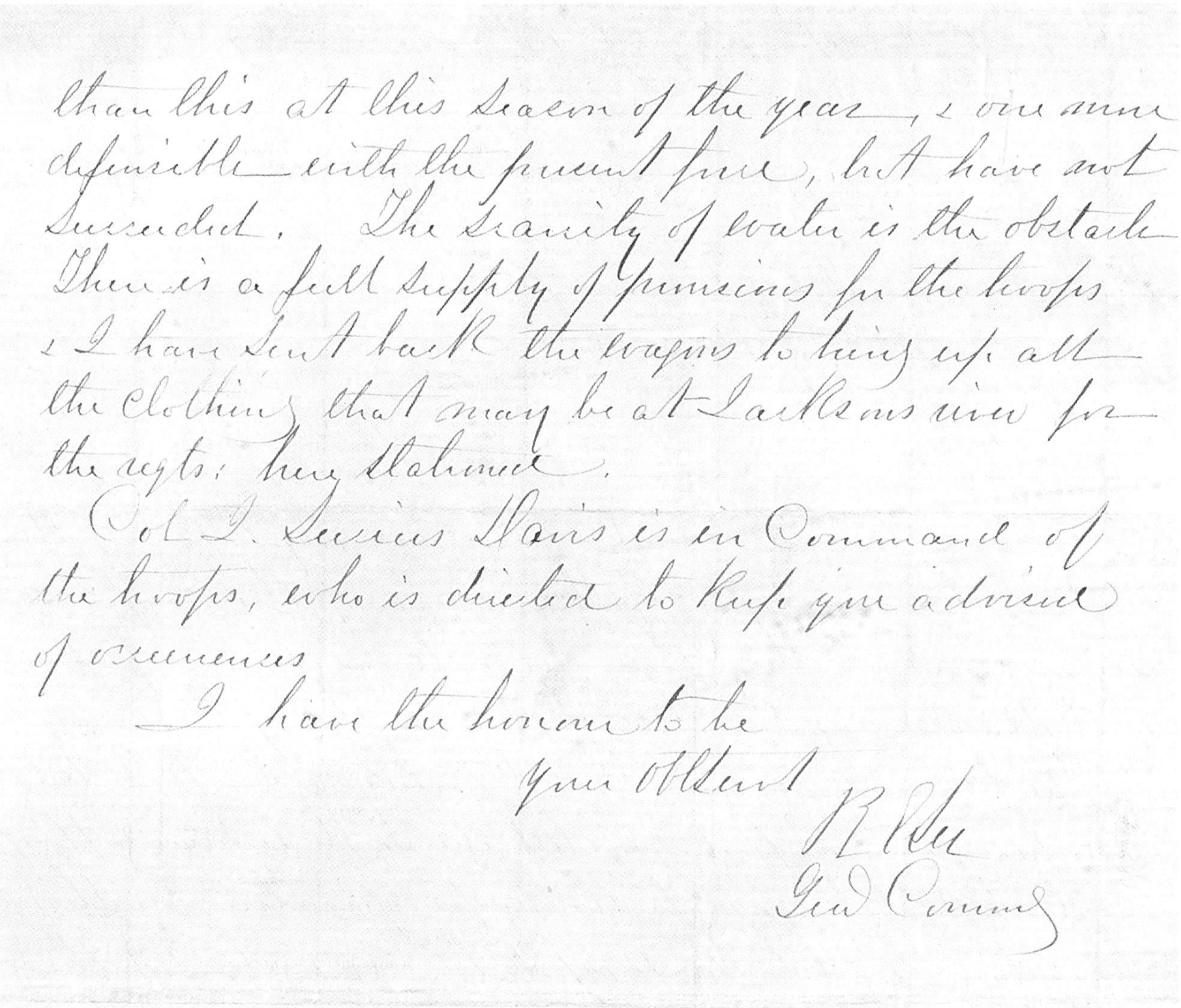

[Handwritten letter reproduced above]

Extract from a letter written by Lee to General John Buchanan Floyd, October 29 1861

This letter was written by Lee in the wake of his defeat at Cheat Mountains, his first campaign of the Civil War.

... than this at this season of the year—& one more defensible—with the present fuel, but have not succeeded. The scarcity of water is the obstacle. There is a full supply of provisions for the troops & I have sent back the wagons to bring up all the clothing that may be at ... for the regts: here stationed.
Col. L. ... Davis is in Command of the troops, who is directed to keep you advised of occurrences.
I have the honour to be
Your Obd Servt
R. E. Lee
Gen Commanding (?)

John Lennon

BRITISH SINGER, SONGWRITER (1940–1980)

John Lennon was born and raised in Liverpool, England. Within a few years he went from playing in a skiffle group in the 1950s to being part of the world's most popular rock group, The Beatles. His controversial romance with Yoko Ono helped lead to the break-up of the band in 1970, after which he began to focus his energies on political causes such as bringing about world peace. Lennon retired from public life after his second son was born, but returned in 1980, when he and Yoko produced their final album, *Double Fantasy*. Shortly afterward, Lennon fell victim to an assassin's bullet in New York City.

Personality overview

Here we see a cool-headed individual whose handwriting lives up to his reputation for an acerbic wit that could easily degenerate into hurtful sarcasm. This is seen in the sharp, pointed strokes and slashing *t*-bars, along with the vertical slant. Despite the somewhat wavy baseline, which reveals moodiness, it was not easy to rattle Lennon, as the emphasis on the downstrokes in this style of printing provides a firm backbone to support his views and opinions.

Relationships

As a general rule, it is more difficult to get emotionally close to printers. They literally break the bonds between themselves and others (the connections between letters) out of a fear of closeness. They prefer to hold other people at arm's length, adopting a more objective way of dealing with them. Lennon could not have been an easy person to live with. Certainly anyone who wanted to be near him would need a thick skin, considering the many downward pointing strokes, such as those in some *t*-bars and the letter *r*, which are made in a stabbing motion. Because these appear in the upper zone, we can assume that they represent verbal "stabbing," or incisive speech.

Intellectual forces

The predominance of straight strokes points to one who used his head to make decisions. He would go with intellect even if his heart told him differently. This doesn't mean Lennon was unemotional. In fact, the heavy flow of ink onto the paper says quite the opposite. However, the intellectual side of his personality was far more developed than the emotional side.

Physical drives

Lennon's writing has a short lower zone, with sharp tics at the bottoms of some letters. The lower zone is one of the areas that helps determine drive and stamina. In this case the contracting of the energy into tics, when it should have been released in the lower zone, indicates someone who would quietly build up his energy then release it suddenly, perhaps explosively.

Motivating forces

The nature of the sample and lack of signature make it difficult to determine Lennon's motivating forces. However, the high level of control evident from the way the page is organized suggests a determination to stick with whatever he undertook.

Between the lines

When applying the principles of Gestalt graphology, analyzing printing such as Lennon's is little different from analyzing cursive writing. The spatial arrangement, which consists of margins and alignment as well as word, line, and letter spacing, is still present, as are other important aspects, such as pressure, speed, and continuity. All these factors can be analyzed, just as in cursive writing, to produce an accurate portrait of the writer's personality.

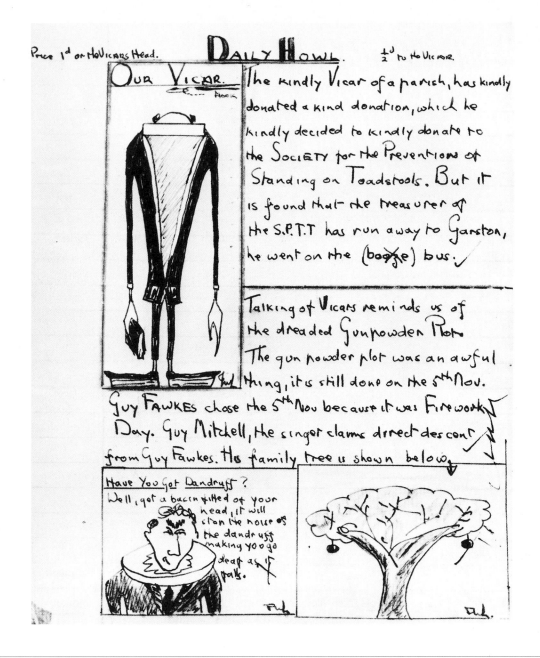

Cartoon scribblings from John Lennon

These nonsense scribblings are part of four such pages.

DAILY HOWL

The kindly Vicar of a parish, has kindly donated a kind donation, which he kindly decided to kindly donate to the Society for the Prevention of Standing on Toadstools. But it is found that the treasurer of the S.P.T.T. has run away to Garston, he went on the (booze) bus.

Talking of Vicars reminds us of the dreaded Gunpowder Plot. The gunpowder plot was an awful thing, it is still done on the 5th Nov. Guy Fawkes chose the 5th Nov. because it was Firework Day. Guy Mitchell, the singer claims direct descent from Guy Fawkes. His family tree is shown below...

Leonardo da Vinci

ITALIAN ARTIST, ARCHITECT, AND ENGINEER (1452–1519)

Leonardo, a genius of immense versatility, was born in Vinci, Republic of Florence (now Italy). At 14 he was probably apprenticed to the leading Florentine sculptor of the time and worked initially as a painter and later as an architectural adviser and engineer. Although many of his works were left unfinished, Leonardo had a profound influence on Renaissance art with paintings such as "Mona Lisa" (1503–1506). He filled notebooks with scientific ideas and diagrams, and his inventive designs included a submarine and a flying machine.

Personality overview

Leonardo's notebooks were mostly written using mirror writing—that is, writing from right-to-left that can be properly read only when held up to a mirror. If we consider that the writing started on the right side of the paper and moved to the left, he left a wider margin at the beginning and a very narrow one at the end. Thus, he was eager to set out on new projects and move swiftly toward his goals. The overall baseline is quite regular, so a firm foundation of security and stability was an important factor. Orderly and organized, he operated best within a structured environment where he knew what to expect.

Relationships

The forms are congenial and rounded. However, the upright slant and disconnections between letters indicate that, while he may have been romantic at heart (given the graceful letter forms), Leonardo would not likely get carried away with his emotions. Rather, he kept a cool head and plenty of social distance. He was not shy, but preferred to be the one who set limits.

Intellectual forces

Although the school model of the day was different when compared to modern ones, the low number of connections from letter to letter in the sample implies independent thinking and a painstaking consideration of new ideas. Leonardo's meticulous nature is evident in the careful return to the baseline of each letter, but again, the low number of connections may reflect his lack of eventual follow-through. Nonetheless, there is a lovely, graceful flow in the writing, an innate grace that can also be seen in the sketches.

Physical drives

The lower zone emphasis indicates an active, lively individual who kept himself busy with a variety of projects. There is a spirit of adventure, but perhaps more on a mental than a physical plane, since the movement does not show very much force. The greatest emphasis is on the downstrokes in the lower zone, which is conserving of energy.

Motivating forces

Underneath his calm, unruffled demeanor, Leonardo's creative originality can be seen bursting out in sudden enlargements of the lower-zone letters and in leaps into the upper zone. The freedom to create is implicit, yet he could also work within a more conventional framework when necessary.

Between the lines

In English we write from left to right. However, left-handed people find it easier to write right to left, as in Hebrew or Arabic, and they sometimes produce mirror writing (words written backward). It is possible to experiment by holding a pen in each hand, starting at the center of the page, and writing your name with both hands at the same time. Mirror writing is the result.

A page from one of Leonardo da Vinci's notebooks

Leonardo kept extensive notebooks in which he made sketches and noted down anything from descriptions of people he saw in the street to designs for a prototype helicopter. In order to protect this information—details of military technology, in particular, would have been highly valuable—Leonardo habitually made his notes in codes that included a curious back-to-front mirror writing, as used here.

Abraham Lincoln

16TH U.S. PRESIDENT (1809–1865)

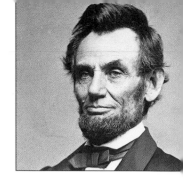

Abraham Lincoln was born in a log cabin in Kentucky and lost his mother when he was just 10 years old. After studying hard, he grew up to become a trusted and successful lawyer in Illinois, earning the nickname "Honest Abe." In 1858 Lincoln ran for the U.S. Senate. He lost the race but earned a reputation for oratory that helped lead to his election to the presidency in 1860. He served two terms, leading the Union through the Civil War, and on January 1, 1863, issued the Emancipation Proclamation, abolishing slavery. On April 14, 1865, in Washington D.C., Lincoln was assassinated.

Personality overview

Lincoln's handwriting, with its strong emphasis on movement, reflects a highly active, progressive individual. There is a loose, flying rhythm, indicative of someone who remained open to new experiences. The fast speed also shows the mental agility of a success-oriented person, one who was impatient to make things happen and willing to do whatever it took to attain his goals. The baseline is straight but flexible, so he was able to make last minute changes of direction when necessary.

Relationships

The genuineness and lack of artifice in the thready openness of the writing indicates that Lincoln was a man who could easily adapt to anyone he met, whether they were a king or a pauper. There are few angles, which suggests an easygoing individual whose congeniality and absence of temper or irritability undoubtedly made him many friends. His signature is simple and congruent with the text, telling us that there was no difference between his public and private selves.

Intellectual forces

For someone who had very little formal schooling, Lincoln's handwriting shows a natural intelligence in the fluid forms and excellent pattern of space. The horizontal movement—evident in the long, strong t-crosses, which are placed at the tops of the stems, as well as in the final strokes that move upward, and the tall upper zone—indicate a man of ambition who set his goals high, though not unrealistically so.

Physical drives

Lincoln had not only the stamina to carry out his objectives but also considerable willpower when it came to directing others. This is shown in the t's, which are long, some pointing downward, all written with consistently firm pressure throughout. The medium-sized middle zone and narrow right margin, meanwhile, indicate a person who was willing to take risks and try new ways of doing things.

Motivating forces

In the strong rightward movement—seen in the narrow right margin, horizontal strokes in the upper zone, and wide, spread out words—it can be seen that Lincoln was future-oriented. A strongly intuitive, progressive thinker, he knew he could rely on his instincts. He was motivated by his ability to look ahead and visualize what might be coming up next.

Between the lines

Rhythm in handwriting is on a continuum from contraction to release. Highly contracted writing is made by an uptight person who is afraid to venture out and try new things. Highly released writing is the opposite—it shows someone who acts with little restraint. Lincoln's loose rhythm is more toward this end of the spectrum. The most desirable rhythm has an elastic quality and is somewhere in the middle.

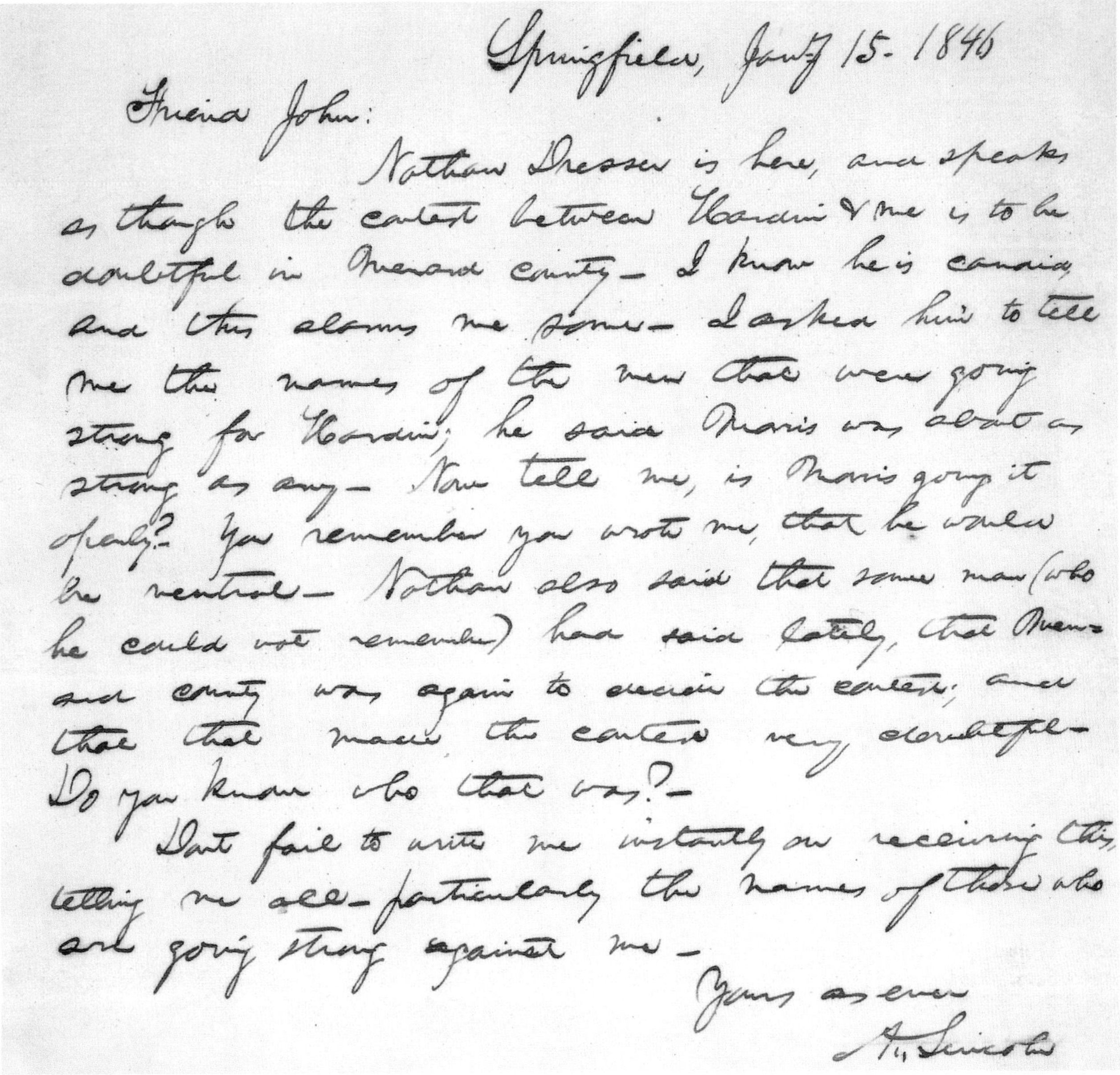

A letter from Abraham Lincoln to John Bennet of Springfield, 15 July 1846

Friend John

Nathan Dresser (?) is here, and speaks as though the contest between ... and me is to be doubtful in ... county—I know he is candid and this alarms me some—I asked him to tell me the names of the men that were going strong for ...; he said ... was about as strong as any—Now tell me, is ... going it openly? You remember you wrote me, that he would be neutral—Nathan also said that some man (who he could not remember) had said lately, that ... and country (?) was again to decide the contest; and that that made the contest very doubtful. Do you know who that was?

Don't fail to write me instantly on receiving this, telling me all—particularly the names of those who are going strong against me.

Yours as ever

A. Lincoln

Louis XIV

KING OF FRANCE (1638–1715)

Louis XIV was only four years old when he ascended the throne in France. Neglected as a child, he became known as the "Sun King" in adulthood, when he was an enthusiastic patron of the arts, theater, and the sciences. In 1661 Louis assumed responsibility for ruling the entire kingdom, a dictatorship he saw to be his divine right. Famed also for building the magnificent Palace at Versailles, Louis had numerous love affairs during his reign, which resulted in many children. He also engaged his country in numerous wars and was both revered and hated at various times during his lifetime.

Personality overview

Louis' handwriting is strikingly angular. Although there are a few curved forms to offset the angles, for the most part he was rigid, stubborn, and unyielding. A tremendous amount of unreleased energy can be seen in the sharp, pointed strokes, and the rhythm is excessively tense, adding to his inflexible nature. This was someone who knew how to get things done by force. His word was law, and once he issued an edict there was no going back.

Relationships

A personal relationship with Louis would have been a stormy one. He despised anyone weaker than himself, yet, while he needed someone who would stand up to him, when they did it could become a battle. The very close spacing impacts on his ability to keep a clear perspective and, when combined with the very strong right slant, indicates someone who could act fast. Despite the intensity of his emotions, the positive side of the angle is the control it confers, so Louis would think before acting.

Intellectual forces

The sharply pointed tops of middle zone letters like *m* and *n*, reveal great intelligence and a curious, analytical

mind. Louis was a quick learner who would never be satisfied to accept someone else's answers to his questions—he had to find out for himself. An abiding desire to dig out the facts and uncover whatever information was available impelled him to investigate to the fullest extent possible anything that interested him.

Physical drives

The tension evident in the angled forms, along with the forceful movement to the right, indicates an extremely active, physically oriented person. Without plenty of physical activity to release it, Louis's energy would build up to explosive levels. The pastose (thick) flow of ink in sharp strokes that point back to the left is a contradiction suggesting that, although he indulged his strong physical drives, he may have suffered feelings of guilt as a result.

Motivating forces

Power was the supreme motivator for Louis. Again, the angles are the dominant form. Lacking any real mitigating connections, it is evident that he had to be in charge at all times. You could say that "arrogance" was his middle name. The large signature adds to the picture of a man who thought a great deal of himself.

Between the lines

The angular connective form illustrated by Louis's script is made in two decisive strokes: up and down. There is no curve, no bending. The same is true in the uncompromising personality of the writer of such an angular script. The angle allows for no release of the tension that builds up in the stroke. There is no flexibility here and, consequently, little resilience either. Anger or frustration in a person is often at the root of this form of handwriting.

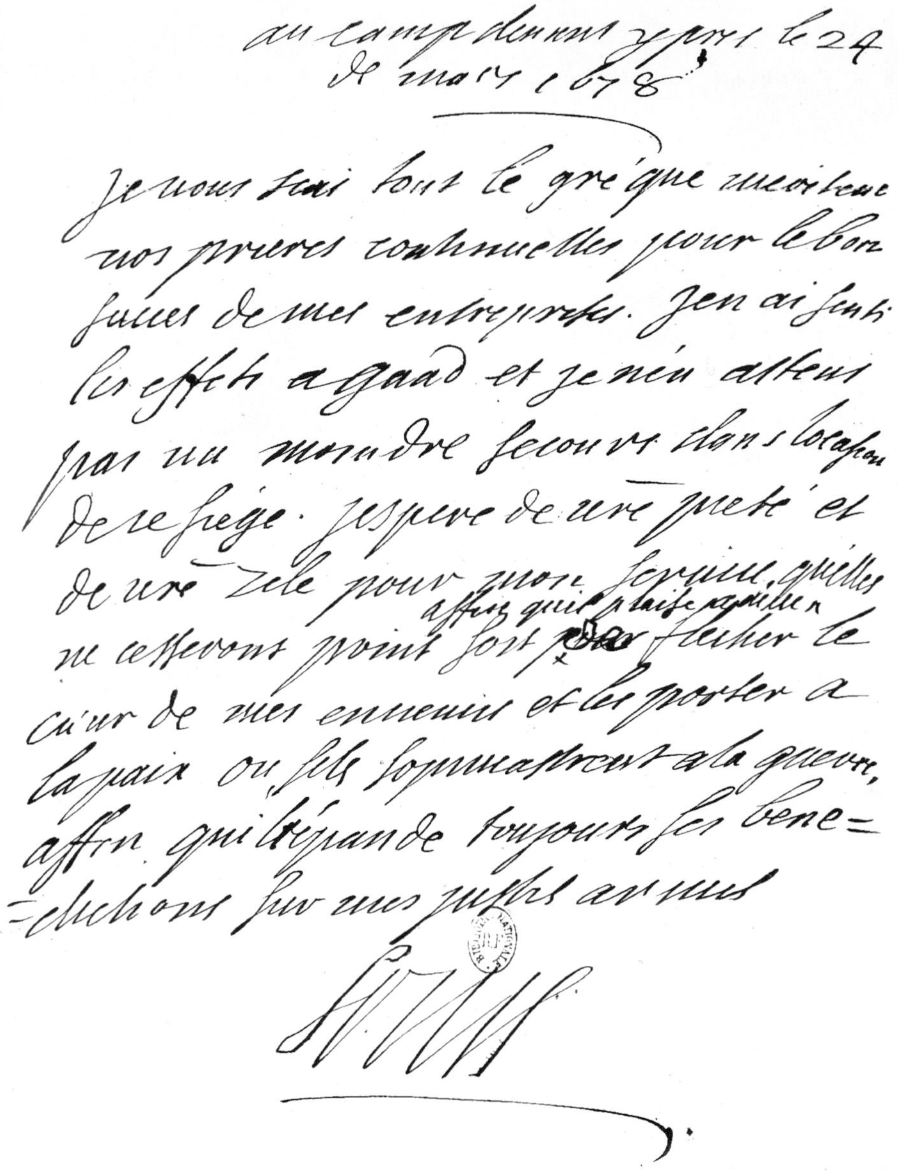

[Handwritten letter in French by Louis XIV]

This letter was written by Louis XIV to Mademoiselle de Lamoignon, 1678

Camp before Yprès, 24 March 1678

I am grateful to you for your constant prayers for my success in my enterprises. I felt their good effects at Gaad [?], and they will doubtless have no less effect in this current siege [before Yprés]. I hope to [have] the pluck and zeal in your service … which will never cease until … I have struck the hearts of my enemies, either carrying them to war … or to peace …

Louis

Paul McCartney

BRITISH MUSICIAN, SONGWRITER (1942–   )

Paul McCartney was born in Liverpool. In the late 1950s he began writing songs with John Lennon and the two formed The Quarrymen in 1956 and The Beatles soon afterward. Arguably the most successful and influential band ever, The Beatles were actually together for only about 10 years. Following their breakup, McCartney formed Wings with his wife, Linda Eastman, and later pursued a solo career. In 1997 he was knighted by Queen Elizabeth II, but the following year saw his wife's death from breast cancer. He has promised to continue speaking out in her name for animal rights.

Personality overview

Paul McCartney's handwriting has quite nicely balanced margins and line spacing, revealing a good sense of where things belong. He organizes his life and time loosely and flexibly, leaving room to make adjustments as a situation develops. The loose rhythm and combination of soft garlands and thread forms suggest a person who knows how to adapt his behavior to get along with others on their level. Although he might stick rigidly to his viewpoint when it is important to him, he would rarely make an issue of more trivial matters.

Relationships

A relationship with McCartney would be low-key and easygoing. The flexible connective forms and lively baseline of the handwriting sample tell us he is likely to go out of his way to keep the peace and avoid confrontations with others. The slant moves in several directions, showing how much he wants everyone to get along and not waste energy on fights or arguments. The moderate pressure indicates that, on the rare occasions when major disagreements arise, he does not bear a grudge or hang on to bad feelings but instead quickly regains his emotional equilibrium.

Intellectual forces

In his writing McCartney strips away most nonessential loops and strokes, leaving only the basics necessary for legibility. This is a sign of a swift, fluent thinker. The writing is open and fast, indicating that his thoughts move along quickly and he is able to gather what he needs for the moment and discard the rest.

Physical drives

Some lower zone letters have a hook on the bottom, indicating unresolved, painful issues that may erupt from time to time in unexpectedly aggressive behavior. The lower zone is often left open and curving to the right. This indicates that McCartney needs someone in his life to make him feel safe and secure, as he seems to have missed out on some of the qualities of nurturing that mothering represents.

Motivating forces

McCartney is motivated not by money or power, but by opportunities to create and make the world a better place. The simplified writing with its released (loose) rhythm says that he does not feel the need to hide who he is but has an open, direct attitude.

Between the lines

Simplification in handwriting, as in McCartney's script, means that the writer leaves off any strokes that are not absolutely essential for legibility. These may include extra strokes on the beginnings or endings of words, loops, and elaborate capitals. People who are able to quickly grasp core ideas often have clear, simplified handwriting. They also tend to be the sort of people who do not need a great deal of preparation in order to get moving.

"Hey Jude"

A page from a notebook showing an early draft by Paul McCartney of the lyrics to "Hey Jude."

HEY JUDE don't make it bad,
take a sad song and make it better
Remember to let her into your heart
Then you can start to make it better

Hey Jude don't be afraid
You were made to go out and get her
The minute you let her under your skin,
Then you begin to make it better

And any time you feel the pain,
Hey Jude refrain, don't carry the world upon your shoulders
For well you know that it's a fool who plays
it cool by making his world a little colder

Hey Jude don't let me down,
Admit your feelings and don't forget her
So let it out and let it in,
Hey Jude begin , bow down to the plasticine banana

Margaret Mitchell

AMERICAN NOVELIST (1900–1949)

Margaret Mitchell, author of probably the best-selling novel of her day, was born in Atlanta, Georgia. While she was attending college, her mother died, forcing Mitchell to return home to work for the *The Atlanta Journal*. In 1926 she retired and began writing her romantic novel about the American Civil War, with its chief protagonist the wild and willful Scarlett O'Hara. Published 10 years later, *Gone With The Wind* sold more than one million copies in only six months. The film of the book, released three years later, won nine Oscars. Mitchell died in a car accident before having the chance to repeat her success.

Personality overview

Mitchell's handwriting is an excellent example of writing in relief, which gives the script a three-dimensional appearance so that it almost jumps off the page. The flow of writing is slightly more controlled than in a completely natural script, resulting in persona writing. This indicates that she cared about her image and worked to make a good impression on others. Additionally, the strong rhythm and form reveal a self-confident person who was not afraid to put herself on the line.

Relationships

The thick, pastose strokes and moderate right slant in a fairly compact picture of space reflect a warm personality. Mitchell was direct and forthright, speaking with sincerity and candor. In fact, she could be brutally honest at times, as indicated in the sharp, pointed strokes and heavy *t*-crosses of the script.

Intellectual forces

The overall rhythmic pattern and well-arranged page attest to an organized mind. Mitchell knew where things belonged and, even though some lower loops touch the tops of the next line, everything had its place. There is a mixture of narrow and somewhat broader upper loops, showing that, while she pushed to broaden her intellectual horizons, Mitchell also found comfort in predictability.

Physical drives

The long lower loops have a reversed pressure pattern, often seen in successful career women. Whereas in a "normal" pattern the pressure is stronger on downstrokes, here we see a sublimation of the sexual energy of the lower zone into the work life of the middle zone. There is a pushing of the pen when it is more appropriate to release the pressure, indicating Mitchell's strong need to control her environment. The heavy *t*-crosses add determination and follow-through.

Motivating forces

The balanced upper zone, in a harmonious picture of space, form, and movement, indicates basic decency. Mitchell took to heart the lessons of her experience and put them into practice to create a personality of symmetry and poise. Her sense of personal pride was important, but the fact that she failed to place a comma after "Love" in the closure (a demand for love), suggests that recognition from others was also high on her list.

Between the lines

A pressure pattern that is not often seen in modern times, except when produced by a fountain or calligraphy pen, is called writing in relief. The downstrokes are thick, but made without heavy pressure, while the upstroke is much lighter, resulting in writing that appears chiseled, like a bas-relief. The implications from this style of writing, seen in this sample of Margaret Mitchell's handwriting, are creativity and a profound appreciation for beauty.

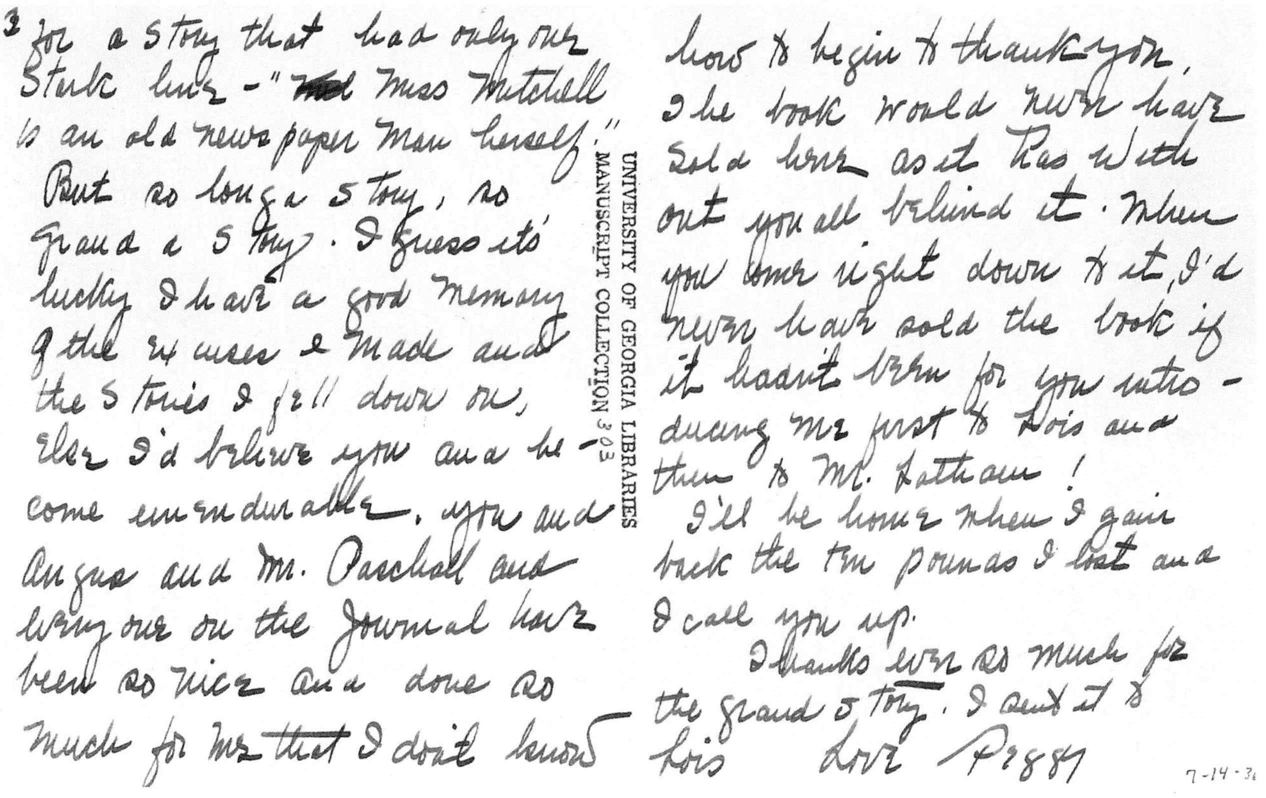

[Handwritten letter, transcribed below]

7-14-36

Extract from a letter written by Margaret Mitchell July 13, 1936

... for a story that had only one stark line— "Miss Mitchell is an old newspaper man herself." But so long a story, so grand a story. I guess it's luck I have a good memory of the excuses I made and the stories I fell down on, else I'd believe you and become unendurable. You and Angus and Mr Paschall and everyone on the Journal have been so nice and done so much for me that I don't know how to begin to thank you. The book would never have sold here as it has without you all behind it. When you come right down to it, I'd never have sold the book if it hadn't been for you introducing me first to Lois and then to Mr Latham!

I'll be home when I gain back the ten pounds I lost and I call you up.

Thanks ever so much for the grand story. I sent it to Lois

Love Peggy

James Monroe

Fifth U.S. President (1758–1831)

James Monroe is best remembered for his contribution to U.S. foreign policy when he issued what later became known as the Monroe Doctrine, a warning to European nations against further colonization attempts in the United States. After distinguishing himself in battle during the War of Independence, Monroe studied law under Thomas Jefferson. His career in politics began quite early and he was elected to the U.S. Senate in 1790. Monroe went on to become president in 1817 and was well known for his honesty during his two terms in office. His administration has been called the Era of Good Feeling.

Personality overview

Monroe's compact writing fills the page. The small, angular forms reveal the implacable personality of one who was willing to keep pushing forward to get the job done, no matter how difficult. Add to that a long, strong lower zone, and we can see persistence and determination. The tall personal pronoun and other well-developed capital letters, attest to Monroe's sense of personal pride.

Relationships

The highly connected writing slants to the right, which is an indicator of a convivial style and ability to interact with others. Although the overall size is small, the word spacing is fairly close. Thus, while Monroe needed social intercourse and would be charming in all circumstances, he would also be discriminating in creating a close circle of friends. Also with the close spacing, he could be subjective in his judgments, letting his heart sway him to some degree when he had to make a difficult decision. Yet, the firmness denotes that his empathy had its limits.

Intellectual forces

The dynamic, rhythmic movement includes sharply pointed middle-zone letters, such as the *m*'s and *n*'s, which signify intellectual curiosity in a mind that was never still. Monroe would look for a common-sense reason before accepting a new idea. His natural style was to link ideas together, as he linked letters together, moving in a logical progression from *a* to *b* to *c*.

Physical drives

Grounded pragmatism can be seen in the long lower zone. It seems that much of Monroe's sexual energy was sublimated into other areas, such as work, as the lower zone is long, but left open. The cradle-like form suggests a strong, unmet need for nurturing and mothering in his early life, and it is likely that later achievements in his career served as a substitute for this.

Motivating forces

The writing is strong and forceful, but in a modest way. A natural leader, Monroe did not know how to take a back seat or sit on the sidelines, and lived by a work ethic that allowed little time for relaxation. The energetic movement, with long *t*-crosses and firm angles at the baseline, is made by someone who eagerly poured himself into all activities and who moved toward his goals with enthusiasm.

Between the lines

The letter *f* is the only letter that passes through all three zones, and it helps determine the writer's sense of organization. The upper loop relates to planning, the lower loop to carrying out those plans. Over-emphasis on the upper loop suggests the writer spends too much time planning, while over-emphasis on the lower loop indicates that he or she may be too quick to act. Sometimes the lower loop of Monroe's *f*'s is bottom heavy, which in this picture shows his need for action.

Part of the Monroe Doctrine, 1823

...nation is devoted. We owe it therefore to candor and to the amicable relations existing between the United States and those powers to declare that we should consider any attempts on their part to extend their ... to any part of the Hemisphere as dangerous to our persons and safety. With the existing colonies or dependencies of any European powers, we have not interfered and shall not interfere. But with the Governments who have declared their independence and ... and whose independence we have, on great consideration, and on great principles, acknowledged, we could not ... any interpositions for the purposes of oppressing them, or controling in any other manner, their destiny, by any European power, in any other light, than as the manifestation of an unfriendly disposition towards the United ...

Marilyn Monroe

ACTRESS (1926–1962)

Norma Jean Baker was raised in a series of foster homes. She later became a photographer's model, which led to a small part in her first movie in 1948. She changed her name and from there her popularity steadily increased until she began to win starring roles in films such as *Gentlemen Prefer Blondes* (1953) and *The Seven Year Itch* (1955). Adored around the world, Monroe married and divorced baseball legend, Joe DiMaggio, in less than a year. She made her final film, *The Misfits*, which was written by another ex-husband, Arthur Miller, a year before her death from an overdose of sleeping pills.

Personality overview

Apparently, this handwriting sample was written while Monroe was a psychiatric inpatient and this would affect her writing according to her emotional state at that time. Despite her obvious anxiety and frustration, the writing is fairly well organized, with a fair spatial arrangement on the page. The most disturbed area is the muddy pressure, which probably indicates some impairment in her moral judgment. From this it can be deduced that substance abuse would have been a likely outlet for her when the stress and pressure became too much. This sample is poignantly reminiscent of another icon who faced similar pressures and challenges during his lifetime, Elvis Presley.

Relationships

At the time of writing, Monroe was clearly trying to live up to an impossible image. This is evidenced by the large capital letters and personal pronoun, *I*, which both reveal an idealized sense of self that has subordinated the "real" self. The otherwise retraced upper zone also sometimes balloons into wide loops, an indicator of the sensitivity she tried to keep hidden from the world but which still pushed its way out.

Intellectual forces

The writing is basically copybook style, so, underneath the glamour, Monroe was quite a conventional person. She felt most comfortable operating within familiar parameters, where she knew exactly what was expected of her. She would probably not have been particularly adventurous or creative.

Physical drives

Monroe's physical orientation can be seen in the thick, heavy strokes and in the long lower loops. She clearly had strong drives and needed to be physically active, while at the same time had the stamina and ability to endure hardships. While her preference was probably to jump in and get started with any particular activity, the tall upper zone suggests that she was also able to plan ahead when necessary.

Motivating forces

The overblown capital letters suggest an intense striving for achievement and recognition. Because the form of the writing is disturbed, we can conjecture that this striving was overcompensation for an ego that had been damaged early in life.

Between the lines

A good analysis requires an adequate sample of handwriting to analyze. An ideal sample, such as this one of Monroe's, consists of the following: a full-sized, unlined sheet of paper, with the handwriting itself written in ink, with a signature. The writer should prepare at least one page, preferably more. The topic is unimportant, but it should not be verse or lyrics. The writer should also state their age and gender, and which hand, left or right, was used.

A letter written by Marilyn Monroe

Dear Lee and Paula

Dr. Kris has had me put into the New York Hospital—pshichiatric division under the care of two <u>idiot</u> doctors—they <u>both should not be my doctors</u>.

You haven't heard from me because I'm locked up with all these poor nutty people. I'm <u>sure</u> to end up a nut if I stay in this nightmare—please help me Lee, this is the <u>last</u> place I should be—maybe if you called Dr. Kris and assured her of my sensitivity and that I must get back to class so I'll be better prepared for "rain."

Lee, I try to remember what you said once in class "that art goes far beyond science"

And the science memories around here I'd like to forget—like screaming women etc.

Please help me—if Dr. Kris assures you I am all right—you can assure her <u>I am not</u>. I do not belong.

I love you both, Marilyn

P.S. forgive the spelling—and there's nothing to write on here. I'm on the dangerous floor its like a cell. Can you imagine— cement blocks. they put me here because they lied to me about calling my doctor and Joe and they had the bathroom door locked so I broke the glass and outside of that I haven't done anything that is uncooperative.

Wolfgang Amadeus Mozart

Austrian Composer (1756–1791)

Wolfgang Amadeus Mozart was born in Salzburg, Austria to a musical family and by the age of six was producing advanced compositions in a variety of forms. A child prodigy, he was acclaimed throughout Europe for his musical ability. In his brief adulthood Mozart produced some of music's most enduring work. However, poor at managing his money, Mozart constantly fell into debt and died a pauper.

Personality overview

Mozart's passion and enthusiasm are evident in the lively movement of his handwriting. The great variability in the size of the middle zone, and the interesting rhythm, reveal an intensely sensitive soul. Add to that the dark color and you have one who experienced life totally through his concrete senses. This could be either a positive or a negative, as it left him vulnerable to his environment.

Relationships

Mozart probably approached his intimate relationships with the same ardor as his music, as the close word spacing, thick strokes, rightward movement and mixed slant suggest. In addition, the baseline is somewhat variable, indicating that he was expressive in his emotions and affections. He needed contact and closeness and it was important for someone to be there for him to hear what he had to say, both musically and verbally.

Intellectual forces

Mozart's mind was never still. The colorful script, with its flying strokes into the upper zone, is symbolic of the way his mind leapt from one creative thought to another. He thought in whole concepts, rather than piecemeal, as seen in the extreme degree of connectedness. That he was able to take those concepts and put them to paper so effectively is seen in the balance of all the zones and in the harmonious flow of the movement.

Physical drives

Boundless energy and drive can be seen in the speed and continuity of the writing, which are a function of rhythm and vice versa. It is almost as if Mozart could not bear to lift the pen from the paper so the ideas he wanted to express would not get away from him. The heavy flow of ink, or pastosity, may be a consequence of the old-style pen or it may indicate a tendency toward overindulgence in alcohol or other substances.

Motivating forces

The original forms, emphasis on movement, and colorful script indicate that Mozart was motivated by his need to create. Nothing was meaningless or small, and he experienced life as fully as possible. His signature was simple and unadorned, telling us that the composition was more important than his ego.

Between the lines

Pastosity is the term used for thick strokes made without heavy pressure, created by a long hold on the pen. With such a hold the pen tip is nearly horizontal to the paper, allowing a copious flow of ink. Both fountain pens and felt-tip pens can produce pastose writing. For a pastose writer such as Mozart, the sensuous, visual experience of handwriting is as important as the text itself.

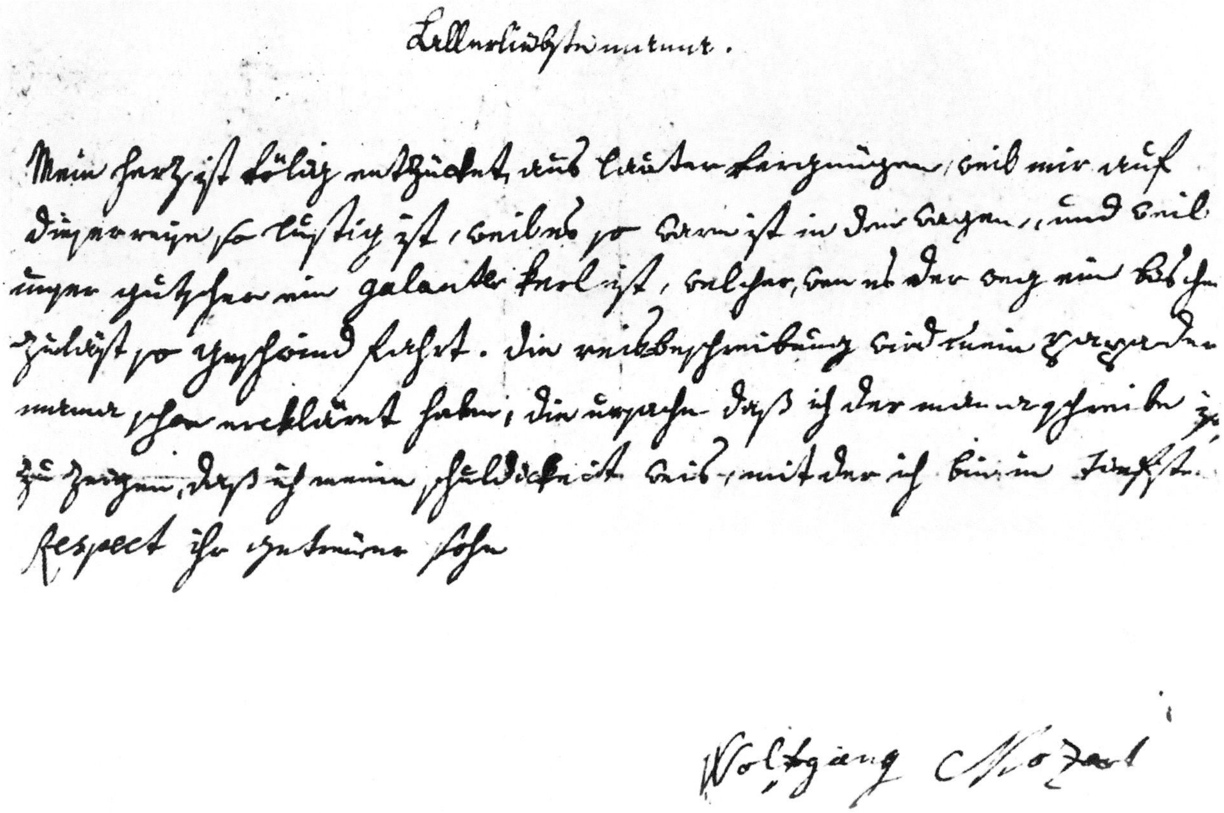

A letter Mozart wrote to his mother, December 13 1769

Dearest Mamma

My heart is completely overjoyed from pure pleasure because this journey is such fun, because it is so warm in the coach, and because our coachman is a gallant chap who, when the road permits it, drives so fast. My papa will have already explained our itinerary to mamma. The reason that I am writing to my mamma is to show that I know my duty, with which I am, in deepest respect, your loyal son,

Wolfgang Mozart

Napoleon Bonaparte

FRENCH GENERAL AND EMPEROR (1769–1821)

An outstanding general, Napoleon Bonaparte rose to prominence in the aftermath of the French Revolution, becoming consul after a coup in 1799 and emperor five years later. He combined legal and educational reforms at home with the amassing of a European empire by war. After defeat in 1814 he escaped from exile but was again defeated by a European coalition at Waterloo in 1815; he spent the rest of his life in exile on St. Helena.

Personality overview
The handwriting has an uncharacteristically delicate look, unlike some other samples of Napoleon's—it may have been that this was a particularly difficult time for him, or that he may have been sick. The extreme uphill climb of the baseline is a sign of one who is fighting against depression. He tells himself that if he can just hold on another day things are bound to get better. Yet there is a constant fear that he is wrong.

Relationships
The tiny middle zone and extreme width between words shows that Napoleon was feeling isolated and alone. Each word is a sandbar in a pool of space, which effectively cuts him off from close contact with others. The small middle zone is in stark contrast to the large capital of his signature, telling us that what he projected to the world was not what he felt inside. This lack of self-confidence was masked by bluster and arrogance.

Intellectual forces
The writing line is light and speedy, showing a quick thinker who used his intuition to his advantage.

However, the same wide spaces between words suggest that Napoleon had difficulty in putting his thoughts together effectively. He could probably spend long periods in silent concentration, working without interruption, but the end result might be a series of discrete ideas that would not always mesh well.

Physical drives
The pressure appears to be quite light, although the extremely heavy underscore below his name belies any weakness. Again, this indicates overcompensation in someone who did not feel as strong or as vital—at the time of this writing—as he would have liked to be seen by those around him. In other of Napoleon's writing samples much greater force and vitality is evident, along with a more rigid adherence to his own viewpoints.

Motivating forces
There is a lot of enthusiasm, at least on a mental level. Even though the writing line is light, every now and then a burst of energy carries him through. In addition, the extra long *t*-crosses carry the mark of Napoleon's need to be in control and give the orders.

Between the lines
Knots and ties are strokes that loop around letters acting as a literal knot or bowtie. These forms can be seen on earlier samples of Napoleon's script and are made by stubborn, persistent individuals who have a hard time letting go of anything. In some cases they may be a sign of extreme secretiveness. Often, knots and ties are seen as double-looped ovals, where they relate to closed communication.

avril le 16 1821 longwood.

ceci est un codicile de mon testament.

1° je desire que mes cendres reposent sur les bords de la Seine au milieu de ce peuple français que j'ai tant aimé

2° je legues au comte Bertrand, montholon et a marchand l'argent, bijoux, argenterie, porcelaine, meubles, livres, armes et generalement tous ce qui m'appartient dans l'ile de St helene

ce codicile tout entier écrit de ma main est signé et scellé de mes armes

Napoleon

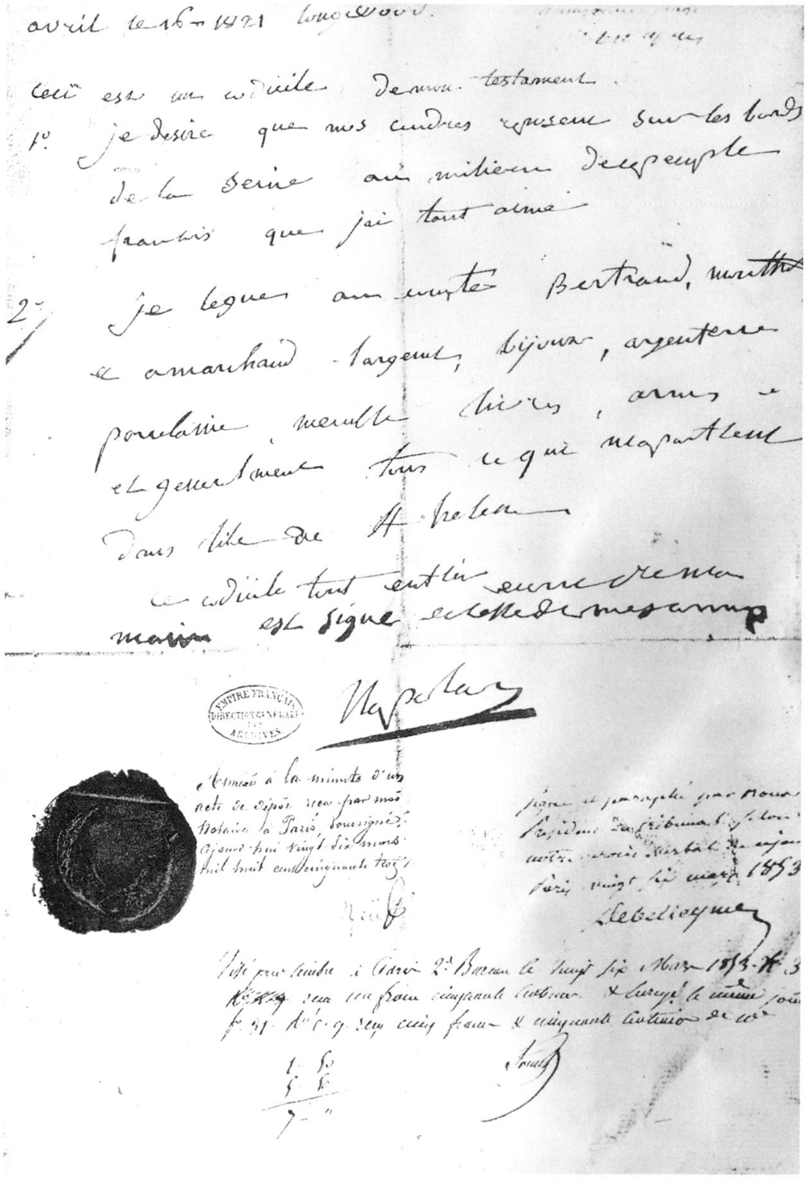

Appendix to Napoleon's will, written in 1821, shortly before his death on St. Helena

The signature and addenda were personally countersigned by several witnesses.

16th April 1821

This is a codicil to my last will and testament.

1) I wish that my ashes repose on the banks of the Seine among the French people who I have always loved.

2) I bequeath to Bertrand, Montholon and Marchand: money, jewels, silverware, porcelain, furniture, books, arms, and everything that belongs to me on St. Helena.

This codicil, which is in my own hand, is signed ...

Napoleon

Lee Harvey Oswald

AMERICAN ASSASSIN (1939–1963)

A high school dropout, Lee Harvey Oswald expressed radical political views from an early age. After three years in the U.S. Marines, he traveled to the Soviet Union where he tried unsuccessfully to become a citizen. After his return to the U.S., and on being refused a visa to go to Cuba, Oswald got a job at the Texas School Book Depository. It was from here that he shot president John F. Kennedy on November 22, 1963. He was himself assassinated two days later. Whether or not Oswald acted alone has since been the subject of much controversy.

Personality overview

Oswald's handwriting is the normal copybook style in a crowded spatial arrangement. This is a sign of one more likely to follow than lead. The cramped word- and line-spacing leave little room for perspective, so his views were based on how things affected him, rather than seeing the bigger picture. On some letters the upper loops fall to the right. Combined with the wavy baseline, which signifies moodiness, abrupt flare-ups of emotion are apparent.

Relationships

Basically a conventional type, Oswald's heavy-looking, muddy writing and narrow lower zone suggest a self-indulgent, but frustrated person, who may have abused drugs or alcohol. The open *b*'s indicate gullibility and, in view of the style and crowded spacing, it is likely he lacked independent judgment. He needed the company of others, but his moodiness probably lost him friends.

Intellectual forces

With the too-tall upper zone and sinuous baseline, Oswald struggled with his sense of ethics. He might have wanted to do the right thing, but was unsure of which path to choose. Often the lower zone does not return to the baseline and the writing is over-connected. Oswald tried to rationalize his emotions through logic, but returned again and again to the past, reliving painful events, rather than resolving them and using the experiences in his day-to-day life.

Physical drives

There is a lot of activity in Oswald's writing but the pressure is blocked, indicating an inefficient use of energy. His frustration is evident in the narrow, often retraced loops. The uphill tendency in this case is not a sign of optimism. With so many words dipping down, it indicates a struggle against depression.

Motivating forces

The overall script is undeveloped and immature, with letters popping up inappropriately in the middle or at the end of words. Oswald could not be counted on to respond consistently, but had a variety of responses to similar situations—blunt one minute, bold the next.

Between the lines

Handwriting reveals information about a writer's past behavior and potential for other behavior. Indicators of pathological behavior, such as the muddy quality of Oswald's writing, are termed by some as red flags. Like everything else in handwriting, red flags must be considered within the context of that particular writing before reaching a conclusion about the effect they may have on the writer's personality.

Letter from Lee Harvey Oswald to the Secretary of the Navy

Dear Sir

I wish to call your attention to a case about which you may have personal knowledge since you are a resident of Ft. Worth as I am.

In November 1959 an event was well publicated in the Ft. Worth newspapers concerning a person who had gone to the Soviet Union to reside for a short time (much in the same way E. Hemingway resided in Paris).

This person in answer to questions put to him by reporters in moscow criticized certain facets of american life. The story was blown up into another "turncoat" sensation, with the result that the navy department gave this person a belated dishonourable discharge, although he had received an honourable discharge after three years service on Sept. 11, 1959 at El Toro, marine corps base in California.

These are the basic facts of my case. I have always had the full sanction of the U.S. Embassy, moscow USSR, and hence the U.S. government. In as much as I am returning to the USA in this year with the aid of the U.S. Embassy bring with me my family (since I married in the USSR) I shall employ all means to right this gross mistake of justice to a boni-fied U.S. citizen and ex-serviceman. The U.S. government has no charges or complaints against me. I ask you to look into this... (continued)

George S. Patton

AMERICAN GENERAL (1885–1945)

George Smith Patton, one of the best known and most controversial U.S. Army officers of recent times, was famed for his command of tank warfare and tough, maverick style. Born in California, Patton followed family tradition, attending military school and making a lifelong career of military service. He distinguished himself in both World War I and II and became known for his discipline, flamboyant style, and impressive abilities in strategic planning. After openly criticizing the Allied denazification policy after the war, he was relieved of his command and died shortly afterward following an automobile accident.

Personality overview

The first impression of Patton's handwriting is of an extremely impatient person who is annoyed at having to take the time to make his thoughts legible. The combination of threads and angles reflects conflict, as these two connective forms are opposites. The angles are a sign of tension, but thread indicates avoidance (of commitment, say). The result was his brusque manner. The well-formed signature suggests that Patton's public image was better than how he saw himself in private.

Relationships

With his "take it or leave it" attitude, Patton would not have been an easy person to live with. The thready writer is unconcerned with communication and really does not care whether his or her message gets across. Patton may have avoided situations that would test his ego, but the angles tell us that, when backed into a corner, he would come out well. He could be a charmer or a devil, whichever suited him at the moment.

Intellectual forces

Patton's writing is linear, with a tall upper zone, signifying someone for whom strategy, theory, and principles were the ruling forces. Considering the unfulfilled lower zone, it may have been that he was able to substitute intellectual achievement for satisfying personal relationships. The speed and extreme simplification of the writing reveal an incredibly fast thinker who seemed to have an invisible antenna tuned to his environment. This allowed him to pick up information needed at the moment, discarding everything else.

Physical drives

The writing speed is extraordinarily fast, the sign of a busy person who feels under pressure to get things done. Patton was active and needed to be in a fast-paced environment where interesting things were going on all the time. He would have soon lost interest in any nine-to-five desk job.

Motivating forces

Patton's motivating force was to create action wherever he went. He could not stand to be idle or see anyone else idle. So his motivation was to motivate others. He was not an easy taskmaster and would not have suffered fools gladly. Anyone reporting to him would have to do so accurately and in a minimum of words.

Between the lines

A writer who fails to choose a specific shape of connective form to link one letter to another produces a thready-looking form. When the writing maintains legibility and is done with pressure this is interpreted positively as a sign of quick thinking. However, when the writing is illegible without noticeable pressure the writer is probably suffering from extreme stress. In Patton's case the illegibility in the middle of words is secondary thread, which means a manipulator and exploiter.

Letter from Patton to Helen __

August 24 '44

My dear Helen:
I apologize for being such a poor correspondent but I have been quite busy.
I had thought that you would be in Europe by now as I asked Jim Arnold (?) to send you.
If and when you get home let us know. We are hard to catch however.
Col Hawkins (?) and Gen. Gray (?) are fine.
Sincerely
G.S. Patton
P.S. We are killing Germans to Hot Hell!

Edgar Allan Poe

American Author, Poet (1809–1849)

Edgar Allan Poe was born in Boston to parents who were traveling stage actors. Orphaned at two, he was sent to live with the Allans, who gave him his middle name but never adopted him. Poe wrote his first known poem, which was never published, in 1824, and went on to eventually become the "Master of the Macabre." His tale '*The Murders in the Rue Morgue*' is considered the first modern detective story. In 1845 his best known poem, "The Raven," brought him fame but not fortune. After years of alcohol abuse, Poe died in Baltimore aged only 40.

Personality overview

The nature of the sample, a poem, probably makes the writing more formal than Poe's normal style. The handwriting is well organized and shows good symmetry in the various aspects of space, form, and movement. There is greater regularity here than in other samples of his writing, and also more linear strokes, indicating unreleased tension. It is known that Poe was a heavy drinker, and he may have needed the release that the alcohol provided. Whatever other effects his drinking had, he generally remained functional. The fairly good spatial arrangement shows that he had enough control to plan his life and time so as to be able to accomplish what needed to be done.

Relationships

Poe's writing is of medium size, with good proportions between the zones. This indicates the more or less conventional outlook of a person who is most comfortable following the standard rules of his social group. The space between the lines is close, but the loops do not interfere with each other. This shows that he allowed others to get close to him and was able to work cooperatively in a group setting.

Intellectual forces

One of the signs of a strong intellect is the sharply pointed letters in the middle zone and a well-developed upper zone. This is a person who would not simply accept what he was told, but had to examine the facts for himself. Poe's handwriting shows intellectual curiosity. Since the upper-zone letters return to the baseline with great regularity, we can assume that he was able to take the information he uncovered and put it to practical use.

Physical drives

The lower zone is long, but not disproportionately so. Poe had strong physical drives that he was evidently able to satisfy in standard ways, as seen in the balanced lower zone letters. Some lower zone upstrokes do not return to the baseline, which suggests that perhaps the trauma of losing his parents at such a young age left a mark that never healed.

Motivating forces

Poe was motivated by his desire to achieve. The many angles, combined with strong regularity and the large capitals in the initials that replace his signature, indicate pride in his achievements and a genuine personality.

Between the lines

Zonal proportions tell us where the energy in the personality is distributed. Middle-zone height is used to determine the proper proportions of other letters, such as middle-zone width, and upper- and lower-zone height and width. The oval letters in the middle zone should be approximately as wide as they are tall, as they are in this sample of Poe's handwriting. Upper and lower loops should also be about twice as tall, or long, as the middle zone height, but only half as wide.

118

To Zante.

Fair isle, that from the fairest of all flowers
  Thy gentlest of all gentle names dost take,
How many mem'ries of what radiant hours
  At sight of thee and thine at once awake!
How many scenes of what departed bliss!
  How many thoughts of what entombéd hopes!
How many visions of a maiden that is
  No more — no more upon thy verdant slopes!
No more! — alas, that magical sad sound
  Transforming all! Thy charms shall please no more—
Thy memory no more! Accursed ground
  Henceforth I hold thy flower-enamelled shore,
O, hyacinthine isle! O, purple Zante!
  Isola d'oro! Fior di Levante!

E A P.

"To Zante"

From a manuscript of Poe's.

Fair isle, that from the fairest of all flowers
Thy gentlest of all gentle names dost take,
How many mem' ries of what radiant hours
At sight of thee and thine at once awake!
How many scenes of what departed bliss!
How many thoughts of what entombéd hopes!
How many visions of a maiden that is
No more—no more upon thy verdant slopes!
No more!—alas, that magical sad sound
Transforming all! Thy charms shall please no more—
Thy memory no more! Accursed ground
Henceforth I hold thy flower-enamelled shore,
O, hyacinthine isle! Oh purple Zante!
Isola d'oro! Fior di Levante!

Jackson Pollock

AMERICAN PAINTER (1912–1956)

Probably famed as much for his painting technique—the radical "drip painting"—as for the actual paintings he produced, Jackson Pollock was born in Wyoming but followed his artist brother to New York in 1930. Here he was apprenticed to his brother's teacher, Thomas Benton Hart. It was not until problems with alcohol drove him to seek help through Jungian analysis that Pollock's style started to become more abstract. He later produced about 50 paintings for the Federal Art Project and by the late 1940s had started on his wall-size "drip paintings." Pollock continued to struggle with alcoholism until his death in a car accident.

Personality overview

Pollock's writing has an aggressive style that stems from the many angles and heavy pressure. The legibility is also impaired by the speed and thready forms, implying that he could not have cared less what others thought of him. If you did not accept Pollock for who he was, then that was your problem. Doing things his way was the only way, and if that meant breaking a few rules, then so be it. The thread/angle combination is made by an exploiter who knew how to capitalize on his resources.

Relationships

The writing rhythm is highly released, which means low self-control and self-discipline. Pollock's demonstrative manner could easily have unnerved more inhibited types. A deep level of sensitivity made his heart bleed when he witnessed injustice. Seeing someone else get hurt was like a personal affront, and just as painful as when he himself was on the receiving end. Yet his changeable nature—as seen in the extreme variability of form, size, and baseline—would make him a difficult person to live with. Those around him would be constantly surprised, not always pleasantly, and long-term commitments were probably not his style.

Intellectual forces

The thready forms and spread-out letter spacing point to someone who was quick to grasp the core idea or concept and could then use his intuition to come up with the right answers. Pollock did not need to participate in an entire conversation to get the gist of what was going on. By combining innovative thinking with common sense, he was able to produce the best results.

Physical drives

The writing reveals restless energy. It is no wonder that Pollock felt the need to walk around his paintings, which he laid on the floor when working on them. The firm movement into the lower zone through heavy downstrokes is a sign of great determination when there was something he wanted to do. Yet there is little release of the energy through an upstroke, suggesting a lack of emotional fulfillment in sexual activity.

Motivating forces

Because Pollock did not feel bound to do things in conventional ways, a whole realm of possibilities existed for him. Autonomy and space were of great importance; without them he would soon become nervous and edgy.

Between the lines

Some graphologists claim that people whose handwriting contains Greek letters, as Jackson Pollock's script does, have a strong interest in cultural pursuits. The Greek *E*, for example, which looks like a backward *3*, is commonly used by Pollock. Other forms are the lyrical *d*, which arcs to the left, and the fluid *g*, which resembles a figure eight. However, many culturally sophisticated people do not choose these letter forms.

Part of a letter written by Jackson Pollock to Sidney James (?)

Sidney James (?) Gallery
15 East 51st St, NYC

Dear Sidney—
*   I think we should feel proud of our first year together. It is unfortunate that we couldn't get the painting back from Europe for the first season. I am glad that you will be in Paris and as my legal agent you will be able to see Mr Michel Tapis (?) or Gabriel-gerard Et Fils—1, Rue Des Italiens—I am enclosing a list of the paintings sent (15) in number and as I have not been paid for any of the paintings supposedly sold I expect all (15) to be returned. Will you thank ... Tapis for his efforts and for sending his book...*

Elvis Presley

AMERICAN ENTERTAINER (1935–1977)

Famed as much for his image and charismatic, overtly sexual performing style, rock and roll singer Elvis Aron Presley changed the face of the popular culture of his day. Presley grew up an only child after his twin brother, Jesse, died at birth. He started out singing church music in Memphis and recorded his first song in 1954. Two years later he had his first big hit with "Heartbreak Hotel," and embarked on a recording and acting career that was to span two decades. After more than 100 hit records, 18 of which reached number one, and 33 films, Elvis died of heart failure due to prescription drug abuse.

Personality overview

The large capital letters signify pride, but the undeveloped middle zone reflects a poor ego. Despite his great success, Presley was not a well-integrated person. The writing is filled with restless activity on a disorganized page. However, while the baseline meanders, the tendency is to move upward, showing his sense of excitement and enthusiasm for the subject matter. The fluctuating height of the upper-zone letters indicate Presley's conflicting feelings about authority figures. On one hand, he had great respect for authority, but that was tempered by resistance to following rules and regulations.

Relationships

The lower zone is malformed and pulls to the left, with hooks, triangles, and a wide variety of forms. Presley was not at all comfortable in this zone, the area of physical urges. The personal pronoun, *I*, gives us a clue, with its odd little loop at the top and downstroke that curves to the left. It shows that he put his mother on a pedestal, and this affected his relationships with women. The left-tending lower-zone letters indicate that although he may have had strong drives, secret feelings of inadequacy undoubtedly led to dissatisfaction in sexual relationships.

Intellectual forces

Presley's emphasis on the upper zone, with it's extra height, indicates a strong interest in the theoretical and philosophical aspects of life. He probably expended a lot of energy exploring the unknown and seeking out alternative realities.

Physical drives

The lower zone is disproportionately long, showing that Presley was extravagant with his resources, spending on impulse. In addition, he needed to be where the action was, and was unable to sit still for any length of time. This combined with his compulsion to engage in adventures—he was excited by the unexpected and this spurred him to try new and different activities.

Motivating forces

Presley was motivated by the need for constant action, as seen in the uncontrolled writing movement and poor rhythm, even if this action did not actually lead anywhere. He thrived on excitement and adventure, without expecting anything more. The wildly variant lower zone also indicates a risk taker who would try just about anything at least once.

Between the lines

The upper zone is the area of mental activity and imagination. Upper-zone elaboration includes extra width, height (as in the extra tall upper loops of Presley's script) or embellishments. Other types of upper zone elaboration are wavy strokes or parts of letters that do not normally belong in this zone. Whether the writer's imagination is used constructively depends on whether or not these embellishments are attractive. In Presley's case they show unrealistic thinking.

A letter from Elvis Presley to President Richard Nixon

During the 1970s Presley asked President Richard Nixon if he could act as an undercover special agent to help deal with the country's drug problems.

Dear Mr. President

First I would like to introduce myself. I am Elvis Presley and admire you and have Great Respect for your office. I talked to Vice President Agnew in Palm Springs 3 weeks (ago) and expressed my concern for our country. The Drug Culture, the Hippie Elements, the ..., Black Panthers, etc do <u>not</u> consider me as their enemy or as they call it the Establishment. <u>I call it America…</u>

Ronald Reagan

Better known today for his time as president during the 1980s, Ronald Reagan's early career was spent as a film actor. During the late 1950s, with his acting career in decline, Reagan's politics became more conservative and in 1966 he was elected, then reelected, governor of California. He went on to win the Republican presidential nomination in 1980 and served two terms as president. His administration was characterized by "Reaganomics," with cuts in taxes and public expenditure, but an increase in military spending.

Personality overview

Reagan's handwriting has a rather casual rhythm, which denotes a congenial disposition. This is someone who goes with the flow and readily accommodates change on a certain level. The *t*-crosses are made with strong pressure, pointing to an ability to direct others through the force of his own will and to see to it that things get done. Many of the *t*-crosses end in a sharp point, an expression of a sharp wit that could degenerate into sarcasm if other controlling factors were not present.

Relationships

The writing line is warm and pastose in a small-to-medium size script. The picture of space is tight, though not overly crowded, and the slant is variable. All this adds up to a basically kindly, conservative, but rather conflicted personality. At the time of writing (1980), Reagan was not sure in which direction he wanted to move and was trying to be a consensus-taker. An examination of other samples over a period of time would reveal whether this lack of direction was situational or a customary part of his personality. He really would like to have pleased everyone if he could. At the same time, the looped upper extension on the letter *p* is said to indicate one who enjoys a good debate.

Intellectual forces

Sharply pointed middle-zone letters such as *r*, *m*, and *n* attest to Reagan's penetrating mind and natural curiosity, both of which could carry him into some interesting places. He would not have been satisfied with readily available facts, preferring to do his own research and analysis. The rounded forms at the baseline suggest some flexibility in considering various alternatives, but common sense would have to play a part in decision making.

Physical drives

Despite the back-and-forth movement of the slant, when an activity or a project really appealed to him Reagan would pursue it with determination. The slackness of the rhythm reveals a more-or-less easygoing nature, which is at odds with the straight initial strokes. These are often made by someone who is defensive and on their guard against criticism, asserting him- or herself if forced to deviate from the chosen course.

Motivating forces

The extra large capital letters reveal Reagan's sense of pride and his desire to achieve. Additionally, the left-to-right movement in the upper zone, seen in the heavy *t*-crosses, denotes a need to lead and direct.

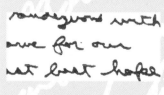

Between the lines

One function of the middle zone is day-to-day relationships and the communication that goes on in them. Middle-zone letters such as *o*, *a*, and *b* should be uncluttered and free of extra loops, hooks, and other contamination. The clearer the oval letters, the clearer the communication. Extra loops may signal hiding, rationalizing, or denial, though the writer is unconscious of this. The ink-filled ovals in Reagan's middle zone signify a love of the good things in life.

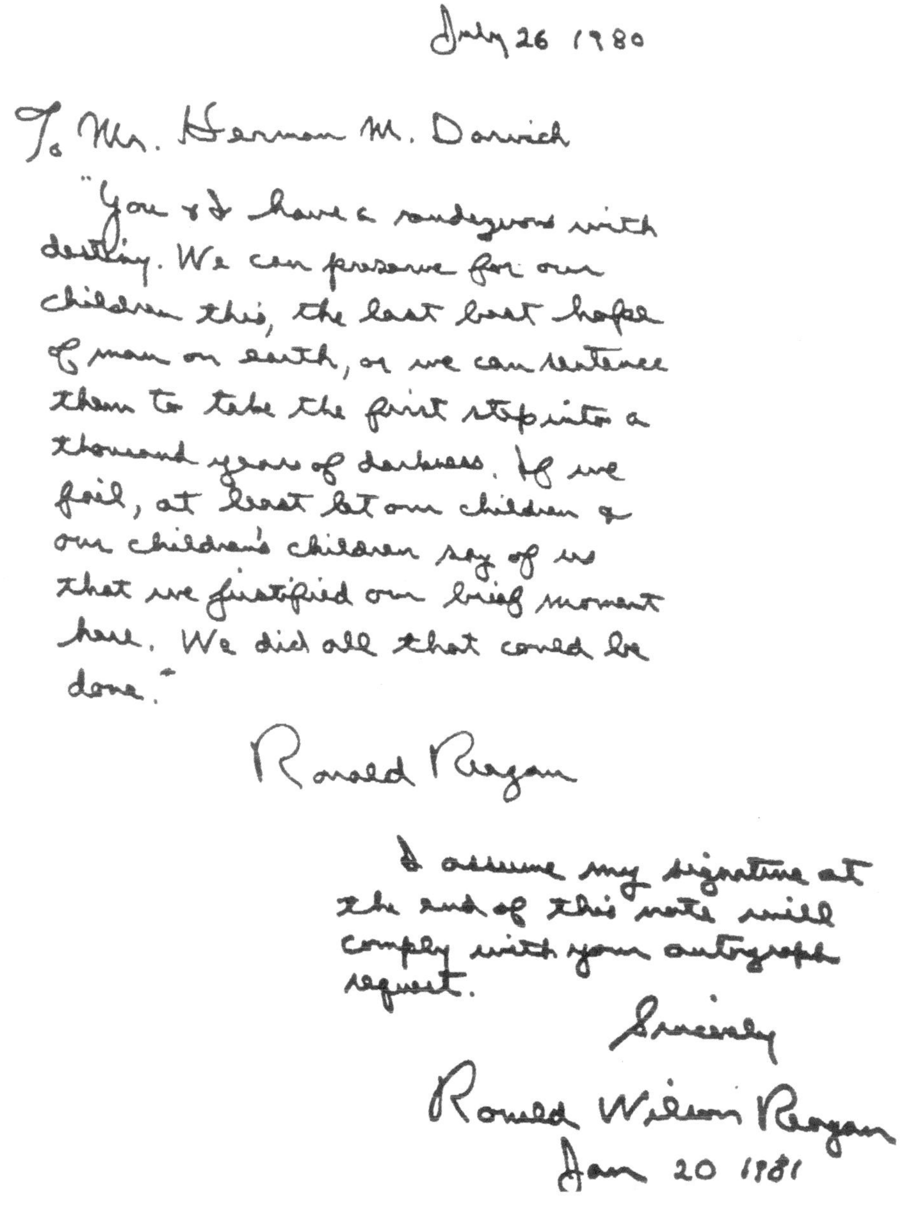

July 26 1980

To Mr. Herman M. Dorrich

"You & I have a rendezvous with destiny. We can preserve for our children this, the last best hope of man on earth, or we can sentence them to take the first step into a thousand years of darkness. If we fail, at least let our children & our children's children say of us that we justified our brief moment here. We did all that could be done."

Ronald Reagan

I assume my signature at the end of this note will comply with your autograph request.

Sincerely

Ronald Wilson Reagan

Jan 20 1981

A letter written by Ronald Reagan to a supporter

July 26 1980
To Mr. Herman M. David
"You and I have a rendezvous with destiny. We can preserve for our children this, the last best hope of man on earth, or we can sentence them to take the first steps into a thousand years of darkness. If we fail, at least let our children & our children's children say of us that we justified our brief moment here. We did all that could be done."
Ronald Reagan

I assume my signature at the end of this note will comply with your autograph request.
Sincerely
Ronald Wilson Reagan
Jan 20 1981

John D. Rockefeller

BUSINESS ENTREPRENEUR (1839–1937)

Born on a New York farm, John D. Rockefeller, Sr. entered the oil business with $2,000 at the age of 20. Only 11 years later he organized the Standard Oil Company, which went on to own or control all the oil refineries in America. In his mid-50s Rockefeller, by then one of the world's richest men, began giving away vast sums of money in philanthropic endeavors in the belief that, "It is every man's religious duty to get all he can honestly and to give all he can." He initiated and supported numerous religious, health, social, and educational programs.

Personality overview

The greatest emphasis is on the upper zone, the area of religion, philosophical thought, and conscience. Rockefeller was a man of high standards, for himself as well as others. The middle zone of the social, concrete world is deemphasized, with energy instead being flung outward, especially into the upper zone area of abstract thought and, to a slightly lesser degree, into the lower zone area of food, sex, money, and the material world.

Relationships

The small middle zone seems to imply either shyness or, perhaps, simply a lack of interest in the social world. Rockefeller used very long final strokes on many words, closing up the empty spaces—a sign of distrust. A propensity for filling up space in this way also shows a compulsive need to control his environment. In the lower zone there are large hooks, which are used to hold on to that which provides security.

Intellectual forces

Even in his mental processes Rockefeller reached down into the lower zone. Witness the very long initial strokes that begin far below the baseline. These "springboard"

strokes are often made by people who have experienced extreme difficulties early in life, and who use these experiences to propel them into success. Also, in words ending with the letter *d,* the letter finishes with a flying stroke in the upper zone. Coupled with the long *t*-bars and the very tall extensions on the letter *p*, this is the writing of someone who felt comfortable in the realm of philosophy. The light pressure and thin ink coverage is often found in the writing of highly religious individuals.

Physical drives

Although some of the lower zone letters return to the baseline, many of them remain as curlicues below the line. Rockefeller's habit of spending time in the lower zone, despite the more spiritual calling of the upper zone, resulted in a conflict between his baser desires and his religious upbringing.

Motivating forces

Rockefeller's motivation seemed to come from promoting his sense of right and wrong. The tall upper-zone letters and large capitals, especially on "God," indicate an intense striving to do the right thing. He could be very hard on himself if he felt he had fallen short of his own standards.

Between the lines

Final strokes on words are the point at which the writer leaves "me" and goes toward "you." He or she moves from one word (him- or herself) toward the next word (another person). The shape of the final stroke implies how the writer approaches the world at large. A blunt final stroke indicates an abrupt manner, for instance, while a very long, curving stroke may be made by one who does not know how to end a conversation. Rockefeller's long final strokes indicated distrust.

A letter written by Rockefeller to his wife, December 20, 1867

Dec 20th 1867

My Dear Wife,

    I arrived last eve at four o'c and after doing some shopping to replace my stock clothing and toilet articles called on Will &
Mira and spent the night very pleasantly. The Christmas presents were burned with the valise and umbrella. Our friends
appreciate them as though rec'd and join in expressions of <u>gratitude</u> that I did not <u>remain</u> in the car with the Baggage, I do
(and did when I learned that the first train left) regard the thing as the <u>Providence of God</u>. I will not by letter rehearse
particulars of the the accident, but hope to ... as early on Wednesday next. Your folks all well, I expect to spend the night with
them. You no doubt rec'd my telegram sent at 6 PM 18th from .... I was <u>well</u> that a good work kept you and Bessie at home.
We certainly should have been in the burned car as it was the only one that went that we could have entered at the time we
would have arrived at the station. I am thankful, thankful, thankful.

    Kiss the darling baby....

Eleanor Roosevelt

DIPLOMAT AND HUMANITARIAN (1884–1962)

Eleanor Roosevelt was born in New York, the niece of President Theodore Roosevelt. She married her distant cousin, Franklin, in 1905 and raised five children. As her husband was recovering from polio she started to become active in public affairs and traveled extensively on his behalf. During her time as First Lady Eleanor was an unprecedented advocate of liberal causes and went on to become one of the most admired, but also most controversial, women of her day. After her husband's death in 1945, she was appointed as a delegate to the United Nations, where she worked tirelessly on behalf of human rights.

Personality overview

Eleanor Roosevelt's handwriting is filled with unflagging energy and drive. There is an almost masculine quality in the dynamic movement. Certainly, there is nothing soft or self-indulgent in the firm, straight strokes. A secure ego is evident in the strong rhythm, simplified capitals, and rightward movement, which show she was not dependent upon the good opinion of others. Her self-belief carried her through the difficult times. The baseline's downward trend seems to suggest that she was feeling somewhat negative, or perhaps fatigued, at the time of writing.

Relationships

The garland connections and strong right slant show that, although Roosevelt cared deeply about others and had an emotional nature, she would not give her friendship indiscriminately. Selective in building a close inner circle of acquaintances, she esteemed her privacy and demanded that others respect it too. To some degree, at least, she might be viewed as secretive and extremely reticent about revealing anything that might be construed as personal. The hooks and circles inside some of the oval letters signify intensely private information that she was reluctant to reveal.

Intellectual forces

While she was a logical thinker skilled at getting to the bottom line of any particular issue, Eleanor Roosevelt also had good intuition on which to call for decision making. The garland forms indicate receptiveness on a social level, but the retraced upper loops imply someone who could be narrowminded and not always willing to listen to new ideas.

Physical drives

The writing exhibits a freewheeling style that suggests someone who was not overly attached to money or possessions. The excellent rhythm and smooth connections demonstrate readiness to adapt, so she could adjust her plans and schedule easily, jumping from one thing to another with a minimum of stress.

Motivating forces

Power and autonomy were strong motivating factors for Eleanor Roosevelt. The overall large writing and tall, simplified capitals reveal a deep sense of pride and self-esteem. There is distinct horizontal movement and moderately heavy pressure that suggest the leadership traits of self-confidence, dynamic energy, and activity.

Between the lines

Handwriting reveals a lot about personality, but some things cannot be conclusively inferred. Among these is gender. Although traditionally "masculine" or "feminine" characteristics are identifiable, it is not always possible to tell whether a sample was written by a man or a woman. Eleanor Roosevelt's writing, for example, is quite masculine—as seen in the linear aspect and dynamic movement. Besides gender, neither age nor handedness can be conclusively determined from handwriting.

Extract from a note written by Eleanor Roosevelt

All ... words to a man than to a woman but the 3 doctors agree he will be eventually <u>well</u> if nothing unforeseeable happens in the next ten days or so & at present all signs are favourable. So we should be very thankful.
Much love
Eleanor
Aug. 18th Love to Betty & Helen ... arrives Aug 31st ...

Franklin D. Roosevelt

32ND U.S. PRESIDENT (1882–1945)

The only president of the United States to be elected four times, Franklin Delano Roosevelt is famed as the architect of the New Deal during the Great Depression and for taking his country into World War II. Stricken with polio in 1921, he worked hard to recover and, encouraged by his cousin, president Theodore Roosevelt, entered politics. He was elected to the presidency in 1932 and brought about sweeping economic reform. Elected to a fourth term toward the end of the war, he died shortly thereafter.

Personality overview

Roosevelt's handwriting puts the emphasis on movement above form and shows that his mind was active and vigorous. His signature, with the increasing size on his surname initial, and the excessively tall personal pronoun, *I*, indicates someone who insisted on being right. In addition, the very tall lead-in stroke on the *p* is the hallmark of one who loves to argue. The simplified forms imply that he could get down to business rapidly without a lot of preparation.

Relationships

It is little surprise that FDR and Eleanor fell in love, as their handwritings are remarkably similar. However, while the large signature made Roosevelt look strong, his ego was actually quite fragile. The middle zone is narrow and poorly formed, which signifies low self-esteem. The tall, narrow upper zone and *t*-bars crossed at the tops of stems are indicative of an authoritarian personality with high standards. He was not an easy person to deal with.

Intellectual forces

The upper-zone emphasis reveals an interest in the philosophical, intellectual sphere, yet Roosevelt was not very open to new information or ideas—as seen in the narrow, retraced loops. His use of simplified forms, such as the *o-f* and *t-h* combinations, show that he was able to see through any extraneous details and make quick decisions.

Physical drives

Despite Roosevelt's physical problems, the writing reveals energy and stamina. The pastosity (heavy ink flow) suggests one who appreciated the finer things in life and he was not averse to indulging, or even over-indulging, in activities such as eating and drinking.

Motivating forces

Roosevelt's need to be in charge is seen in the large signature and personal pronoun and, given the tall extension on the *p* and long *t*-crosses, he would brook no interference from others.

Between the lines

The personal pronoun, *I*, reveals important information about how the writer views him- or herself, and also how he or she views the early relationship with their parents. When the top loop of the *I* is made first, that loop represents "mother" and the bottom loop "father." In reverse, with the bottom loop made first, then the bottom loop represents "mother" and the top loop, "father." Roosevelt's *I* shows that he put his mother on a pedestal, while his father was in some way absent.

130

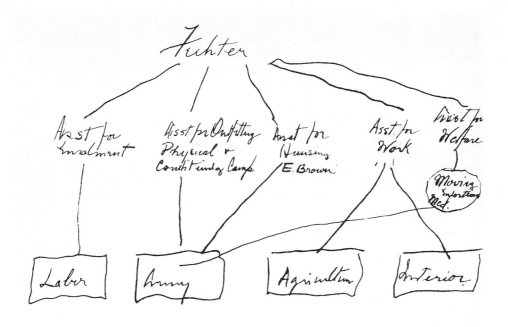

Franklin D. Roosevelt's organization of the Civilian Conservation Corps

This concept of the organization of the Civilian Conservation Corps was written sometime in early 1933.

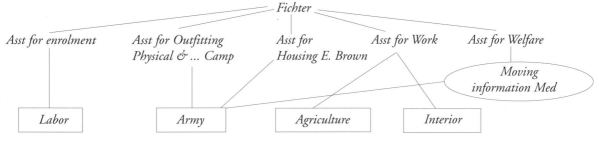

I want _personally_ to check on the location scope etc of the camps, assign work to be done etc.
FDR

Ernest Shackleton

ANTARCTIC EXPLORER (1874–1922)

Ernest Henry Shackleton was a British explorer famed for his expeditions to the Antarctic, first as part of Captain Scott's epic journey (1901–1904) and three years later as leader of the *Nimrod* Expedition. Born in Ireland, Shackleton completed his education at Dulwich College and entered the mercantile marine. Some years later he joined Scott's Discovery Expedition to the Antarctic, but poor health forced him to leave the group. He returned to Antarctica in 1907 on board the *Nimrod* but ice prevented the expedition from reaching its goal. He was nonetheless knighted on his return.

Personality overview

The writing moves swiftly across the page, looking as if Shackleton was in such a hurry to get his thoughts down that he barely presses into the paper. Despite the somewhat impaired legibility, he was feeling enthusiastic and ready to approach the next challenge. There is a great deal of adaptability in the spread-out garland forms, which allowed him to accommodate change without trouble.

Relationships

Although he could be romantic when he wanted to be, Shackleton was probably not the sort to reveal his innermost feelings. There is a conflict in the extreme right slant—indicating that he cared about people—and the wide spaces between words, which kept him isolated. The straight downstrokes with no loop suggest that he expressed his physical needs in a direct manner. Most likely, though, with the return strokes in the lower zone either cut off or returning to the right in a counterstroke, his drives were often left unfulfilled.

Intellectual forces

Shackleton thought exceptionally quickly, which allowed him to move swiftly from one idea to the next and so respond to any challenges as they arose. There are few breaks within words, and some words even connect, showing an immediate comprehension and ability to apply what he learned to new situations.

Physical drives

The pressure appears to fluctuate, an indication of one who needed to conserve energy. This is possibly because Shackleton had lower stamina than was needed to meet his objectives. His biological imperatives, that is, the need for food, sex, money, and material goods (as seen in the lower zone of writing), were not particularly strong. In fact the lower zone is deemphasized when compared to the middle zone, and he probably expended more energy in carrying out his daily plans.

Motivating forces

The desire for progress and independence were big motivators for Shackleton. The rapid speed of the writing, open spaces between letters and words, and the stick form of the capital *I* make it clear that he refused to be hemmed in by time, space, or supervision. He was a man who thought for himself, made his own choices, and then acted upon them.

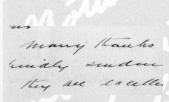

Between the lines

Pressure (depth) is the third dimension of handwriting. When examining a photocopy it is impossible to determine the degree of pressure, although light/dark patterns are sometimes easier to see. The normal distribution of pressure is heavier downstrokes and lighter upstrokes, although sometimes the opposite is true. The light pressure of Shackleton's script (combined with the rightward movement) suggests his need to move forward despite a lack of stamina.

A letter written by Shackleton in October 1904

22.10.04

My dear Gilmour
Many thanks to you for so kindly sending me the photos, they are excellent.
I am very busy now arranging for our new session but will be able to be down at the Savage (?) Club on the 5th.
With kindest regards to your wife.
Yours v. sincerely
EH Shackleton

O.J. Simpson

AMERICAN ATHLETE (1947–   )

Orenthal James Simpson, once a professional football player legendary for his evasiveness and speed, is probably better known today for the car chase and trial that followed the murders of his ex-wife and a friend. Simpson began playing football in high school. He won the Heisman Trophy in 1968 and the next year was the number one draft pick of the Buffalo Bills. He set many records during his football career, but retired in 1979 to become a sports commentator and actor. In 1995, he was found not guilty of the murders of his ex-wife, Nicole, and her friend Ronald Goldman. A subsequent court judgment found him liable.

Personality overview

Block-style printing is an all-middle-zone style of writing, which signifies involvement in the present. The writer has little interest in what happened yesterday and is not concerned with planning ahead. Such a writer is a highly verbal person who focuses on what is going on at the moment and acts on it. The strong degree of variability in this writing—changing slant, baseline, letter form, size, and margins—are an indication that Simpson was suffering enormous conflicts at the time of writing. This is natural, as the sample was written shortly after his ex-wife's death and while under medication.

Relationships

The middle-zone emphasis is used by an egocentric person who needs the spotlight. Therefore, in a personal relationship Simpson would expect his partner to put many of her own needs aside in favor of his. The variable slant and baseline are the hallmark of a moody person who can suddenly become emotional. The changing style, from block capitals to upper and lower case print, seems to suggest different behavioral styles. With the last letter of many words growing larger, this is someone who literally insists on having the last word.

Intellectual forces

Simpson is a pragmatic thinker who is more interested in taking care of the here and now than spending a lot of time on philosophical thought. There is not a lot of upper-zone activity and the squared letter forms indicate that he focuses on the practical needs of daily life, so he may have some difficulty seeing the big picture. The printing in a wide spatial arrangement suggests someone who wants to make sure he is absolutely clear in what he wants to get across.

Physical drives

There is energy and motion in the writing sample, but it does not seem to be going anywhere. The back-and-forth movement effectively prevents any real progress from taking place. This is suggestive of someone whose physical drives are the controlling factor in his life, rather than him controlling them.

Motivating forces

Simpson is motivated by his need for security at a rather basic level and that includes survival needs. Again, the subject matter of the sample and the time of writing are likely to have affected the handwriting.

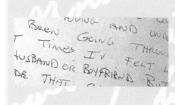

Between the lines

A wide spectrum of variation exists in handwriting. At one end is the extremely regular, mechanical writing of someone so uptight that they cannot release their feelings without exploding. At the other is extremely irregular writing where there is little or no consistency and the writer acts on every impulse. Simpson's writing is more toward the irregular end of the spectrum. A moderate degree of variation shows a normal degree of expressiveness and self-control.

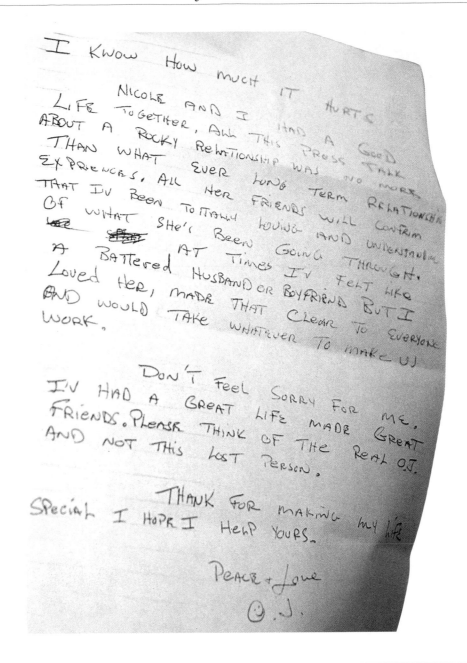

A letter written by O.J. Simpson in June 1994

This is the last page of one of three letters written by Simpson and read on June 17, 1994, by friend Robert Kardashian during a news conference.

I know how much it hurts

Nicole and I had a good life together, all this press talk about a rocky relationship was no more than what ever long term relationship experiences. All her friends will confirm that I'v been totally loving and understanding of what she's been going through. At times I'v felt like a battered husband or boyfriend but I loved her, made that clear to everyone and would take whatever to make us work.

Don't feel sorry for me. I'v had a great life made great friends. Please think of the real O.J. and not this lost person.

Thank you for making my life special I hope I help yours.

Peace & Love

O.J.

Joseph Stalin

RUSSIAN DICTATOR (1879–1953)

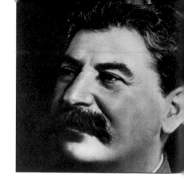

Joseph Stalin was born the son of a Georgian shoemaker and studied for the priesthood before being expelled for promoting Marxism. He joined the Bolshevik Party in 1903 and in 1922 became secretary-general of the Communist Party. On Lenin's death in 1924, Stalin overcame his rivals to become the most important figure in Soviet politics. His social reorganization of the Soviet Union caused millions of peasants to starve when he seized their grain and sold it to promote urban industrialization. He maintained his dictatorial rule until his death, using his secret police to purge the army and the Party of any opposition.

Personality overview

Stalin's signature contrasts sharply with the body of his writing, indicating a conflict between the ruthless ambition he showed to the world and the lesser degree of self-confidence he felt in private. The large capital S, which looks like a C in English, is made in a covering gesture, with the t hidden inside the curve. It is much larger than his first name, which is shown as simply an initial, effectively hiding reference to his personal self. The S rears up, reflecting a competitive, power-hungry attitude.

Relationships

There is a sinuous quality to the baseline and some strokes pop up unexpectedly, almost sneakily. This is someone who could appear quite charming when it suited him, but who would then attack from behind. The uneven letter size, in conjunction with the heavy flow of ink and extra-strong slant to the right, along with the letters that pop up out of the middle zone, lead to the conclusion that this was a man who often acted inconsistently, reactively, and explosively.

Intellectual forces

The emphasis on the middle zone at the expense of upper- and lower- zone height suggests a self-involved person whose own interests would always come first. The angles show Stalin's mind was alert and curious, and the fast speed of the writing is that of an agile thinker. Yet the muddiness would act as a braking force to slow him down, indicating a suspicious and distrustful nature.

Physical drives

The writing has strong emphasis on movement in a compact picture of space, showing the writer to be highly active. Overall, the writing is muddy, with pointed tops on letters that should be curved, signifying a high degree of tension. The muddiness also reveals a damming up of basic drives and urges; when the dam broke, those drives would flood out in a torrent of frustration.

Motivating forces

Stalin's handwriting, with its accent on heavy pressure, angular forms, and close spacing, reveals a controlling person who had to have things his own way. The signature, with its large capitals and heavy angles, adds to the conclusion that he was motivated to seize power any way he could. Fear drove his behavior, fear that if he did not control all space, as seen in a crowded picture of space within wide margins, someone else would attempt to control him.

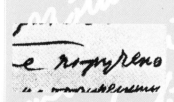

Between the lines

There is a phenomenon in handwriting known as shark's teeth. This is an angle form with a curve, where the first upstroke curves backward and the downstroke bows outward, so that it looks like a shark's tooth. It can be seen in the middle of the word highlighted here in Stalin's script. Shark's teeth tend to indicate someone who behaves cunningly, smiling to your face while calmly stabbing you in the back.

Уважаемый
Кирилл Афанасьевич!

Дело, которое поручено Вам, является историческим делом. Освобождение Ленинграда, сами понимаете, — великое дело. Я бы хотел, чтобы предстоящее наступление Волховского фронта не разменялось на мелкие стычки, а вылилось бы в единый мощный удар по врагу. Я не сомневаюсь, что Вы постараетесь превратить это наступление именно в единый и общий удар по врагу, опрокидывающий все расчеты немецких захватчиков.

Жму руку и
желаю Вам успеха

И. Сталин

29.12.41.

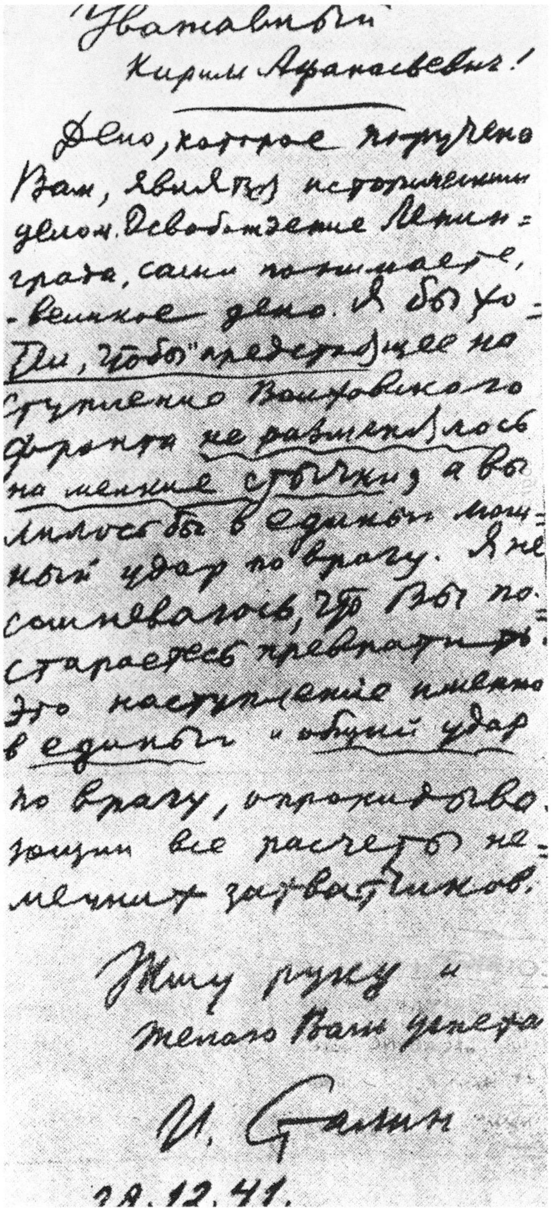

Stalin's message to K. Meretskov, Deputy People's Commissar of Defence, Dec. 29 1941

Dear Kirill Afanasyevich!

The task which is given to you is a historical one (event). As you understand the liberation of Leningrad is a great event. I would like that the future main attack in the Volkhov area (front) wouldn't splinter into small pieces but would turn into one strong (massive) blow to the enemy. I have no doubts that you'll try to do your best to make this blow as strong as possible to destroy the plans of the occupying Germans. I shake your hand and wish you success.

Y. Stalin

Note: Y is J in Russian Cyrillic.
Note 2: Kind thanks to Dr Ze'ev Bar-Av for his feedback and contribution to the discussion regarding Stalin.

Mother Teresa

MISSIONARY (1910–1997)

Albanian-born Agnes Gonxha Bojaxhiu went to Ireland to join the Institute of the Blessed Virgin Mary when she was just 18. It was here she took the name Teresa, for Little Teresa of Lisieux. Six weeks later the young nun traveled to India, initially as a teacher but later requesting permission to work with the poor in the slums of Calcutta. After studying nursing, Mother Teresa moved into the slums and founded the Order of the Missionaries of Charity in 1948. Numerous centers were opened by the order to help the blind, lepers, cripples, and the dying. Mother Teresa received the Nobel peace prize in 1979 for her work.

Personality overview

Mother Teresa's handwriting reveals warmth and compassion. The large writing size may partly have been a result of her poor eyesight, but the well-shaped, round forms and pastose (thick) strokes attest to a fullness of feeling and a sense of fun. The writing tends to move uphill, despite dipping down at the ends of some lines, which suggests an innate optimism in the face of difficulty. She knew how to use her sense of humor in order to get what was needed.

Relationships

This is someone who enjoyed the public eye and was at her best when able to use her cleverness—seen in the unique forms and strong horizontal movement—to achieve her goals. The round, full letters are a sign of a strongly emotional nature, one who cared deeply about people and who felt everything they felt. Some middle zone letters stretch out wider than they are tall, indicating that she sometimes took on more than was reasonable.

Intellectual forces

Advanced age and poor health is suggested by the shakiness in some strokes, but Mother Teresa was bright and intelligent. The emphasis is on the middle zone, so people and the social aspects of life were more appealing to her. Nonetheless, the upper zone is tall and wide enough to allow for new ideas and innovative thinking.

Physical drives

Deemphasis on the lower zone is common in people who have chosen a religious life. Their focus is less on the physical and more on spirituality. This can be seen in a very tall upper zone or, as in Mother Teresa's script, in an emphasis on the middle zone of practical, day-to-day activities. The self-discipline evident in the strong *t*-crosses, combined with the solid, dark strokes, indicates strength of purpose in one who was willing to work long and hard to attain her objectives.

Motivating forces

Mother Teresa had great determination and an ability to seek out the material necessities that made life easier for those to whom she ministered. Witness the hooks at the ends of words and final strokes plunging into the lower zone. Although she was not without conflict, seen in the variable slant, her chief motivation was love, manifest in the large, rounded forms and firm rightward movement.

Between the lines

Middle-zone height symbolizes how tall a person feels (their ego strength). When middle-zone letters such as *o*, *a*, and *m* are measured from top to bottom, the standard middle-zone height is 3mm. Generally, an average middle-zone height reflects the writer's conformance to society's norms. Taller than 3mm, as in Mother Teresa's script, shows an individualist, although in her case it may signify poor vision. Shorter than 3mm, by contrast, reflects a more retiring person.

A message handwritten by Mother Teresa and given to A.P. Monday October 16, 1989

Mother Teresa was admitted to Calcutta's Woodland Nursing Home on September 5 following cardiac problems. She was released October 14.

... kindly thank the people of the whole world and the woodland people for all their prayer and tender love and care I have received. God bless you.

Teresa

Dylan Thomas

WELSH POET AND WRITER (1914–1953)

Although he did poorly in school, Dylan Thomas's first volume of poetry, published when he was just 20 years old, won him much critical acclaim. His work was known for its romantic, complex imagery, its pathos and its humor, but Thomas was also notorious for his reckless drinking bouts. He made numerous reading tours of the United States but remained troubled by a turbulent marriage, financial problems, and excessive drinking. Thomas died after a drinking bout shortly after completing one of his most famed works, *Under Milk Wood* (1954).

Personality overview

There is in Thomas's handwriting a gentle, sweet quality that suggests a rather modest, somewhat shy person, as seen in the slight left slant and many breaks between letters. He was more comfortable moving inward, not from a lack of self-confidence but simply because he was happier working alone, without interruption.

Relationships

The warm, colorful strokes and flexible letter forms suggest someone who got along well with people. However, the lower zone is cramped and the spaces between words are wide, suggesting that Thomas did not have a strong need for interaction in large groups. He would have been perfectly content to socialize with one or two carefully selected others who shared his interests.

Intellectual forces

There are some wonderful connections into the upper zone, showing Thomas's leaps of creative imagination and ease with the theoretical world. The interesting joinings of many *t*'s to the next letter show a quick grasp of new ideas and an ability to express them eloquently. Although the rhythm is uneven, the overall good picture of space indicates that Thomas knew where things belonged in life and was able to keep a clear perspective. Not surprisingly, he uses the lyrical *d*, sometimes adopted by poets. The combination of printing and cursive in a positive script shows an ability to work with what he had in order to create something entirely new.

Physical drives

Although Thomas had the determination and persistence to do what he needed to, as seen in the blunt down-strokes into the lower zone, his chief focus was not on physical activity. The heavy flow of ink indicates a low degree of self-control in one who overindulged himself in certain areas of life.

Motivating forces

Thomas was motivated by his need for harmony. The pattern of light and dark strokes and attractive, simplified forms reveals one who would not be able to tolerate a chaotic, noisy environment for long. In fact, such an atmosphere could impact on his emotional equilibrium to the point of making him physically ill. Thomas needed to be where his senses could be stimulated, surrounded by natural beauty.

Between the lines

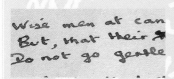

Small writing such as Dylan Thomas's—that is, where the middle-zone height is less than 3mm—reflects a modest person with little interest in being in the limelight. A sense of personal accomplishment is much more rewarding for this writer than public acclaim. He or she is an introvert who recharges his or her emotional batteries by going inward for reflection, in contrast to their extroverted counterpart, who is rejuvenated by interacting with others.

A very early working draft of "Do Not Go Gentle Into That Good Night"

Dylan Thomas's poem addressed to his dying father.

Do Not Go Gentle Into That Good Night (pray)

Do not go gentle into that good night,
Old age should dance & rave at close of day;
Rage, rage against the dying of the light.
Wise men at candle and know dark is right,
But, that their hearts had not burned fierce & gay,
Do not go gentle into that good night.
Good men, the last wave by, crying how bright
Might their grave times have sailed in the green bay,
Rage, rage against the dying of the light.

And the last vain, but, as they
The last wish vain, but, as they die away
Do not go gentle into that good night.
But though they know
But that they had wrestled fierce & gay
But that...

Donald Trump

AMERICAN REAL-ESTATE MOGUL (1946–)

Donald Trump was born in Queens, New York, the son of a wealthy real-estate developer. After graduating from New York Military Academy, Fordham University, and the Wharton School of Finance, where he placed first in his class, Trump went to work for his father and began acquiring properties. He built Trump Tower, bought a football team, an airline, and two beauty pageants, and sponsored boxing matches and co-authored books about himself and his accomplishments. By 1990 he was facing bankruptcy, but with the rebounding economy was able to turn his financial affairs around and continues to enjoy success.

Personality overview

The bold, block-printed writing style, with its strong pressure and firm movement, reveal independence and the need to march to his own drum. Single-mindedly focusing on his objectives, Trump pours his energy into achieving his goals. He is not easily discouraged, but has the determination and willpower to delay the moment of triumph until the time is right. Even when the outlook is bleak, he refuses to give up or become downhearted for very long.

Relationships

The close spacing suggests that Trump can be responsive to the needs of the others in a group and probably likes getting together and collaborating as a team member. However, this is only the case so long as he feels he is not being taken advantage of. It is likely he also enjoys spending time on his own, pondering the group discussion. Trump knows how to get his needs met by being direct and candid about what he wants.

Intellectual forces

The sharply pointed *m*'s and *n*'s show an analytical nature. As one who carefully evaluates everything, Trump takes problems apart piece by piece, examining each element in meticulous detail. The steady baseline says that he will not do anything unless there is a pragmatic, common-sense reason for him to do so.

Physical drives

The squared forms, strong pressure, even baseline, and methodical movement show that Trump selects activities in his life that help move him toward his goals. He lives by a work ethic that does not allow for much free time. Nonetheless, the pastose flow of ink indicates his appreciation for the trappings of a comfortable lifestyle. As a consequence, he focuses on obtaining the kind of money he knows is necessary for him to enjoy that lifestyle for as long as possible.

Motivating forces

The regularity in size and slant reveal Trump's strong drive for achievement and need to set his own agenda. His entrepreneurial spirit does not mind failures because he is aware that they bring him closer to success. His strong self-esteem and self-confidence can be seen in the tall capitals—Trump is not afraid to let others see that he feels good about himself.

Between the lines

A moderately uphill baseline usually signifies an upbeat attitude while a downward tending one suggests someone who is depressed or feeling down. However, an uphill baseline can also signal a fight against depression. The writer is continually pushing him- or herself to keep going, trying to remember that tomorrow is another day, if he or she can just hang on a bit longer. In Trump's case the steep baseline is actually symbolic, representing as it does the design of Trump Tower.

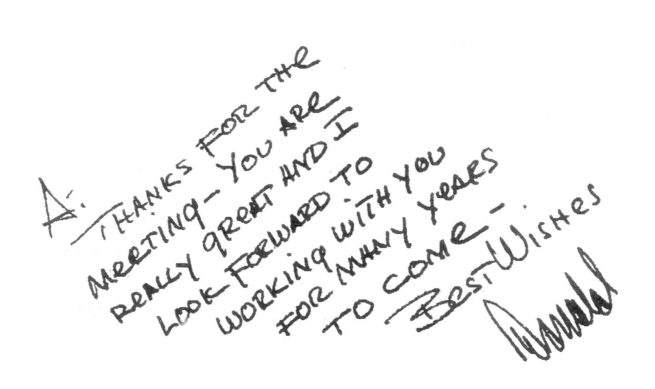

A note written by Donald Trump

A.—
Thanks for the meeting. You are really great and I look forward to working with you for many years to come.
Best wishes
Donald

Queen Victoria

BRITISH QUEEN AND EMPRESS (1819–1901)

Queen Victoria, the daughter of the Duke of Kent and Princess Victoria of Saxe-Coburg, ascended the throne at the age of 18 and was queen for 64 years, the longest reign in British history. With her beloved Prince-consort, Albert, she bore nine children. Following Albert's death in 1861 Victoria spent the rest of her life in mourning. Although many technological and humanitarian strides were made during her reign, she became unpopular with her subjects and survived several assassination attempts before dying of natural causes.

Personality overview

One of the most remarkable aspects of Victoria's handwriting is the secondary horizontal expansion. Although the words themselves are quite expanded, the individual letters are narrow, revealing a basic introvert who learned how to act in an extroverted manner. The strung-out quality of the middle zone suggests that she was under great stress at the time of writing. The middle zone is almost flat, while the lower zone is very long, which demonstrates a desire to avoid the realities of the daily routine and escape into lower zone activities of food, sex, and material things. Victoria was probably not the austere woman that history and the term "Victorian Age" would have us believe.

Relationships

The overall size of the writing is quite small, betraying a serious, practical person who might not welcome a lot of social activity. The long, straight final strokes often have a hook or dot at the ends, which have the effect of holding off others, preventing them from coming too close. Nonetheless, the right slant shows intense emotional responsiveness, so this is a person who could feel deeply when she cared for someone.

Intellectual forces

There are some inventive connections from the middle to the upper zone, a sure sign of a nimble mind. Although she was basically a logical thinker, Victoria was also intuitive and resourceful, able to make leaps of logic and find new ways of looking at things. The writing is speedy and shows impatience with those who could not keep up.

Physical drives

The long plunges into the lower zone demonstrate intense physical drives, yet despite their length the loops are narrow and sometimes stay open, rather than crossing at the baseline. This shows that Victoria was frustrated in her intimate life. Her tremendous energy may have been sublimated to the necessary activities of daily life, despite attempts to avoid them. That the ends of lines tend downward suggests depression and discouragement.

Motivating forces

Victoria was forceful and expressed her power through the large capitals and strong horizontal movement. The extremely long *t*-crosses are made by someone who would brook no interference when she gave an order. There would be no doubt about who was in charge.

Between the lines

Horizontal expansion refers to the degree handwriting moves to the right. It reveals how much elbow room the writer requires. A broad expansion indicates a refusal by the writer to be restricted in time, space, or any other way. When the expansion is caused by narrow letters with wide spaces in between them (secondary expansion), as is the case with Victoria's handwriting, this shows that the writer is basically shy but has learned to act in an extroverted manner.

A letter written by Queen Victoria to Wellington

Osborne
April 11, 1848.

The Queen must write a line to Field Marshal the Duke of Wellington in order to express to him personally her high sense of the service which he has again rendered to his sovereign & his Country on the occasion of the expected riots. The arrangements seem to have been most perfect & to have inspired the whole of London with complete confidence.
The Queen was pleased to hear of the hearty way in which the Duke of Wellington was cheered wherever he showed himself.

George Washington

FIRST U.S. PRESIDENT (1732–1799)

George Washington, first president of the United States, was born into a wealthy family in Virginia. He fought in the French and Indian War, and in 1775 was elected commander of the Continental Army. For six years of war against the British, Washington commanded his army under some appalling conditions. He took the oath of office as first president of the Republic on April 30, 1789, and served two terms before retiring to his plantation.

Personality overview

Washington's handwriting is simple and unpretentious, neat and carefully executed. This denotes an ability to think and speak clearly, to get one's thoughts across in plain language. There is a soberness about the writing, which indicates a pragmatic, down-to-earth character, someone who took life seriously. The left margin tends to move slightly rightward, while the right margin seems to crash into the edge of the page for a few lines, which indicates great enthusiasm for what he is writing about.

Relationships

The strong right slant in the upper zone is mitigated by the more moderate downslants in the middle zone, a sign that, while Washington may have been quick to respond on a mental level, he would not act on his first impulse without considering the consequences. The clear, simple script means that anyone who was close to Washington knew that they could count on him to keep his promises and commitments. The tall upper zone of the sample indicates the high principles and standards he expected of himself.

Intellectual forces

The writing is mostly connected, breaking where appropriate, a sign of a logical, sequential thinker. The upper zone is tall, with properly proportioned width, so Washington had an interest in intellectual pursuits and sought constant mental challenges. Since the lower zone also has adequate length, we can infer that he was willing and able to put his ideas to practical use.

Physical drives

The writing moves purposefully across the page, with a well-developed lower zone, showing good stamina and endurance. He could follow through on projects once begun, and functioned well in both planning and acting on his plans. He was not daunted by obstacles—when they got in the way he would simply roll over them.

Motivating forces

The arcade connective form is a sign of Washington's respect for tradition. Along with the tall upper zone this suggests he was motivated by his principles to help create a framework within which others could operate.

Between the lines

The left and right margins represent the writer's view of the past and the future. The amount of space at the start of the left margin reveals whether he or she clings to the past or, like Washington, is enthusiastic about the future and beginning new projects. The width of the right margin shows whether the writer is able to sustain this level of enthusiasm or becomes cautious and pulls back.

A letter written by Washington when commander of the Continental Army

Head Quarters 4th April 1778

Sirs
I have received your letter of the 27th Feby. informing me of your having letters from Doctor Franklin, and that you are desirous of serving in the Continental Army—it will save you unnecessary traveling and expences to apprise you that Congress alone can place you there, and consequently that your personal application to them, is the first step to be taken by you in prosecuting this business—if they should determine in your favor, it will give me pleasure to render your Situation in the army as agreeable as possible—
I am Sirs
Your most obedient and most humble Servt.
G. Washington

James Whistler

AMERICAN ARTIST (1834–1903)

A leading artist of his day, famed for his portraits and paintings of London at night, James McNeill Whistler attended West Point for a time but soon gave up the army to pursue his art. In 1855 he left America to study in France, and spent a number of years traveling in Europe, painting in oil and watercolor, and doing etchings. In Paris he won acclaim with his painting "Symphony in White No. 1: The White Girl" (1862), and it was around this time that he began living in London. Often short of money, the outspoken and bohemian Whistler was a much talked-of and often controversial figure in London society.

Personality overview

Whistler's handwriting is well organized, with highly original forms in a balanced picture of space and movement. The thready quality of the script implies the "take it or leave it" attitude of a nonconformist who lived in his own world, making up his own rules as he went along. An extremely independent individualist, Whistler probably viewed himself as the only voice of authority. The angles that appear among the threads indicate that he was not hesitant about expressing that view.

Relationships

With the openness of the writing field, Whistler was extremely perceptive and aware of the moods and feelings of those around him. However, he was also an idealistic and highly critical person, which is reflected in the *t*-crosses at the tops of or above the stems, and in the sharply pointed strokes. Although sophisticated and refined in his intellect, Whistler was a perfectionist, so was probably quite a difficult person to live with. In addition, he was quite selective about those with whom he would share his time, so admittance to his social circle was a rare privilege.

Intellectual forces

The writing moves so fast that legibility is impaired and the reader is forced to read very carefully in order to understand what is being said. Whistler was impatient, did not suffer fools gladly, and had no patience for listening to, or giving, long explanations. While he had a talent for tackling complex problems, he had no patience either for the mundane. His only concern was the goal at hand, not how he would reach it, and he would drive himself until he had completed his chosen task.

Physical drives

With the deemphasized lower zone, Whistler's focus was chiefly on mental pursuits, and it seems unlikely that he would expend a lot of energy on physical activity. The warm, pastose strokes are reminiscent of Claude Monet's handwriting, and reveal voluptuous tastes. He was one who appreciated the trappings of the good life.

Motivating forces

Whistler's need to express himself creatively seems to be the greatest motivating factor. As in all other areas of his life, he chose his own unique forms of expression.

Between the lines

The writing impulse refers to the effort that begins when the writing instrument touches the writing surface and ends when the instrument is raised, even if momentarily. In a handwriting sample it is possible to measure the writing impulse pattern by placing tracing paper over the text and tracing each movement from start to finish. The resulting series of lines and dots demonstrate the rhythm of the writing. Whistler's writing impulse is very mixed and choppy, shown by the variable degree of connectedness between letters.

A letter written by James McNeill Whistler to David Croal Thomson, July 1895

David Croal Thomson, manager of the Goupil Gallery, acted almost as a personal agent to Whistler. The letter defends the manner of his signature (a "butterfly" design) on his paintings and goes on to discuss Whistler's hope that no painting of his remain in England.

> *... Be good enough to say to Mr McCulloch (?) with my compliments that the picture is signed—as completely as one of his own cheques is signed when he has written his name upon it.*
>
> *If not content with that, he ... asked to print it in the "bottom right hand corner," the nature of his own request to me, may become clear to him.*
>
> *I have, as you know, my own...*

Oscar Wilde

IRISH PLAYWRIGHT (1854–1900)

The child of two Dublin literary talents, Oscar Wilde distinguished himself at Trinity College, Oxford, where he won the Newdigate Prize for his poem "Ravenna." Self-consciously aesthetic, eccentric, and intellectual, Wilde found literary success with social comedies including *The Importance of Being Earnest* and *Lady Windemere's Fan*. Publicly accused of the crime of sodomy, Wilde elected to face a trial he could have avoided, and was sentenced to two years in prison, an ordeal later recorded in *The Ballad of Reading Gaol*. Left bankrupt and socially ruined, he moved to Paris where he died in obscurity.

Personality overview

The wide spatial arrangement is most noticeable, followed closely by the almost painfully simplified letter forms. The extreme simplification reflects Wilde's enthusiasm for aestheticism, as he strips away every extraneous stroke, leaving only the bare essentials needed for legibility. The soft letter forms and loose rhythm reveal a sensitive, tender-hearted romantic who craved harmony.

Relationships

That Wilde needed a great deal of space in which to operate is clear. The space between words is so extreme it is as if the individual words served to emotionally and physically isolate him. Wilde might have felt shut out from the world, unable to open the door that would allow him to feel more connected. However, the middle zone letters are not squeezed but full, so this self-isolation was by choice. Too much closeness would have left him feeling emotionally overextended. The lower zone moves rightward in a counterstroke, then ends to the left in a large hook, demonstrating Wilde's attachment to men. It was difficult for him to trust others, which might have caused some to view him as snobbish until they got to know him.

Intellectual forces

The many disconnections between letters are smooth, and leave room for flashes of genius. Every unnecessary stroke is stripped away, so Wilde was a concise, even incisive communicator who used an economy of words to convey an idea. His intellectual curiosity, seen in the unusual letter forms, allowed him to mold reality to suit himself.

Physical drives

The open lower zone suggests unfulfilled sexual needs, as well as a need for security. The cradle form is made by those who have not received the nurturing they needed early in life. The overall wide spatial arrangement indicates a desire for luxury, but wastefulness with one's resources. The upward pointing baseline indicates that Wilde worked at keeping a positive mental outlook and sense of humor.

Motivating forces

An original thinker who followed a unique path, Wilde created innovative answers to the challenges that confronted him. Motivated by his need for intellectual freedom, he did not feel bound by conventional expectations, but marched to his own drum.

Between the lines

The amount of space left between words is an indicator of how much social distance the writer chooses. The standard width is the size of a letter *m* in any particular handwriting. A person who writes his or her words very close together demonstrates a need for a great deal of social contact. By contrast, a person who leaves wide spaces between words, as Wilde does, shows a greater need for distance and space away from others.

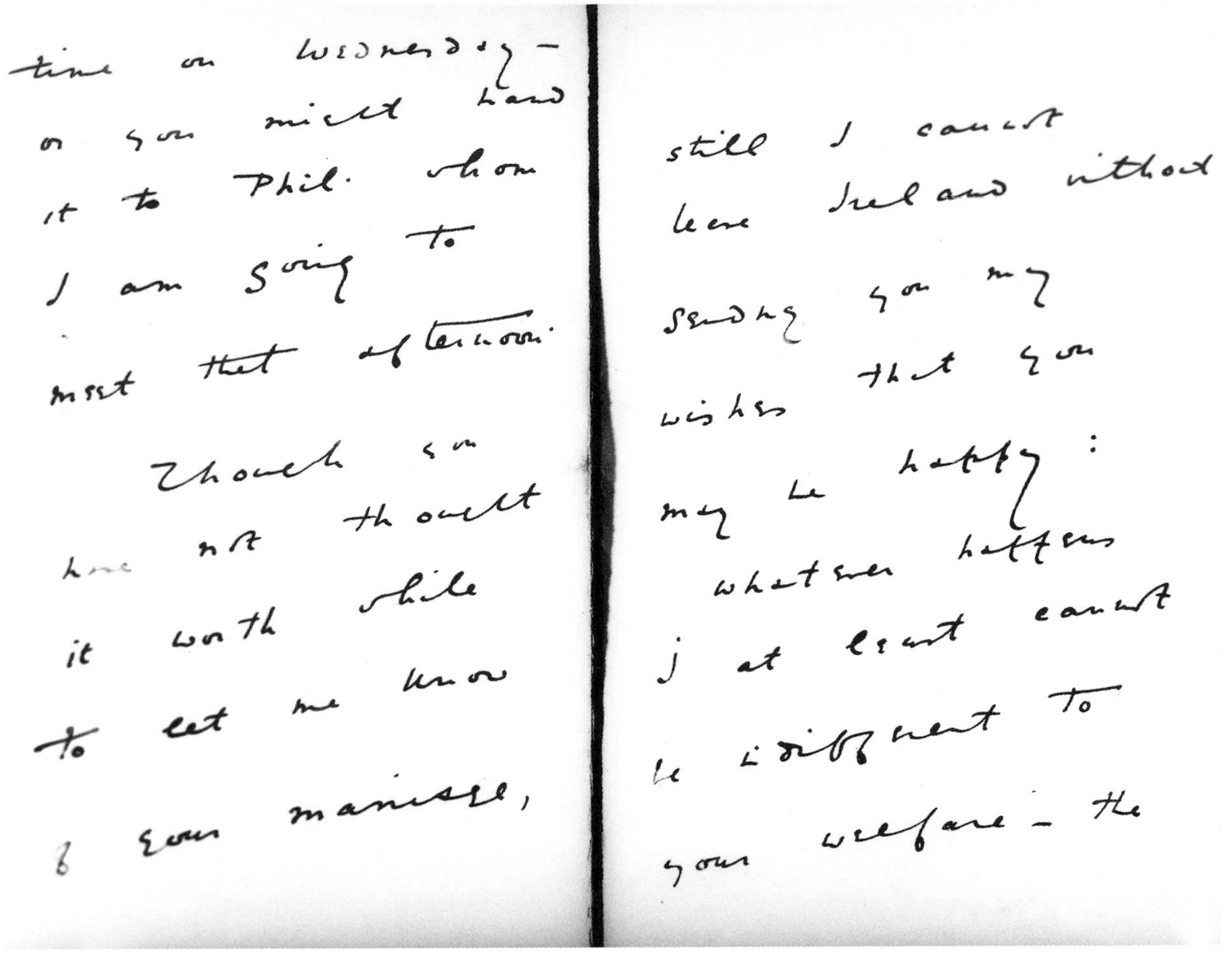

[Handwritten letter facsimile]

Extract from a letter written by Oscar Wilde

.... time on Wednesday—or you might hand it to Phil whom I am going to meet that afternoon.

Though you have not thought it worth while to let me know of your marriage, still I cannot leave Ireland without sending you my wishes that you may be happy: whatever happens I at least cannot be indifferent to your welfare—the ....

Virginia Woolf

ENGLISH NOVELIST AND CRITIC (1882–1941)

Virginia Woolf, one of the most original novelists and important critics of her day, moved to London after the death of her father. Here she became a leader of the Bloomsbury set, a modernist literary movement. In 1912 she married Leonard Woolf and together they founded the Hogarth Press. A feminist, Woolf wrote about the challenges facing women writers of the time. She was also known for her stream of consciousness writing style, such as in one of her best-known novels, *To the Lighthouse* (1927), and for exploring her characters' innermost thoughts. Woolf suffered recurring bouts of mental illness and drowned herself in 1941.

Personality overview

Woolf's handwriting reveals an extraordinarily intelligent person whose chiseled strokes remind one of a bas–relief. There is an obvious pattern of light and dark in a script where angles dominate. Sharply analytical, she examined cause and effect to the *n*th degree, using a dry, sardonic humor to express her views. It is unlikely that Woolf would have appreciated a compliment as knowing she had done her job well would be praise enough. Likewise, she would have been unlikely to give praise to others.

Relationships

The wide spaces show that it was difficult for Woolf to receive from others, as she closed herself off. There is a judgmental quality in the distance between the words, which mirrors the distance she kept between herself and other people. The angular writer is absolutely loyal, and expects the same kind of loyalty in return. If someone disappointed Woolf, she was unlikely to forgive.

Intellectual forces

The many narrow, angular forms are made by a person of very definite views, views that would not necessarily conform with those of society. Woolf created her own standards and expected others to meet them. And always, she would be ready to argue her point. Although there are some curved forms, they are relatively few, a sign that she was not easily influenced once she had made up her mind. The upper zone is tall and mostly retraced, so she would not have been willing to listen to suggestions.

Physical drives

Woolf would not choose the easy way forward. Again, the angles are uppermost, denoting a habit of leading with her chin and taking up one challenge after another. She would have nothing but scorn for those who chose the softer option. The lower zone shows firm down-strokes, a sign of determination. However, there are also hooks at the bottoms of these downstrokes, which signifies frustration and hidden anger.

Motivating forces

The writing is sophisticated and shows good taste and cultural development in the attractive, original forms. With the lower-zone hooks and generally angled script, it appears that Woolf sublimated her sexual drives into her work. The narrowness of the letters also shows introspection, a need to explore the inner dimensions of her soul.

Between the lines

Proponents of the Gestalt method of handwriting analysis view handwriting as a whole entity, made up of space (intellect), form (ego), and movement (energy). If one or two of these areas is overly exaggerated, it shows a lack of personality integration. The area that stands out the most will show how the energy of the personality is being directed. So, for example, the emphasis in Woolf's writing is on movement, with angles shooting upward and a nervous, agitated quality.

Part of a working draft of Woolf's novel *Mrs. Dalloway*, published in 1925

The events of the novel take place in a single day, and are punctuated by the chimes of Big Ben.

Eight ... Big Ben, nine, ten, eleven; & then with a ... of finality, though presumably the strokes were accurately spaced ... the last no more emphatic than the first twelve.

Always that—always that mystery that fascination that Glimpse withdrawn. But whose fault was it, she asked, as Big Ben began striking. One, two, three; and she was extraordinarily happy. She felt no pity for the young man who had killed himself; nor for his wife; nor for herself; nothing but pride; nothing but joy; for to hear Big Ben strike three, four, five, six, seven, was profound & tremendous, hearing too as she stood there, motor hoot & bus pant, & then some sudden strange cry; while behind her in the drawing room, people chattered, shouted, laughed; she must go back; she must breast her enemy; she must take her rose (?). Never would she submit—never, never!
Eight, Big Ben struck, nine, ten, eleven; ...

Wilbur Wright

AMERICAN AVIATION PIONEER (1867–1912)

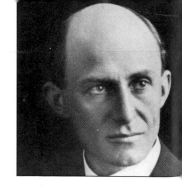

Wilbur Wright, working with his brother, Orville, financed his early inventions and aeronautic experiments with the proceeds from a bicycle shop. The brothers built their first flying machine, a biplane kite, in 1899 after observing the flight of buzzards. Four years later they designed and built their first powered machine, the *Kitty Hawk*, and it was this that made the first unassisted, sustained airplane flight. After obtaining a contract to build airplanes for the U.S. Army in 1908, Wilbur began performing exhibition flights in France. He remained a bachelor all his life, flying being his greatest passion.

Personality overview

Wright's handwriting is more or less the school model of the time, with some simplification. This is an indication of a conservative, modest personality, someone who did not wish to stand out in a crowd. At the same time, the writing runs into the right margin with such abandon that he is forced to turn the letters downward in order to complete some words. This happens as his self-discipline begins to weaken, and he warms to his subject. Wright's enthusiasm becomes more apparent as he proceeds.

Relationships

The mostly connected writing with a strong rightward slant is evidence that Wright was a sociable person who knew how to interact with others. However, the high degree of angles and the very tall extension on the letter *p* suggest that he could easily become dogmatic and argumentative when trying to make a point. He was serious and tense much of the time, and probably found it hard to relax and enjoy himself.

Intellectual forces

The middle zone is deemphasized in favor of the upper and lower zones. Wright had little interest in the mundane, daily routine of life, preferring to expend his energy on mental pursuits. The carefully formed, round *i*-dots, which are close to the stem, demonstrate his compulsive attention to detail. The firm, horizontal movement, as seen in the long *t*-crosses, indicates that Wright was goal-directed and set his sights at reasonable levels. A logical thinker, there is enough horizontal expansion for us to conclude that he was open to new ideas and had the mental resources to experiment.

Physical drives

Angular writing is a sign of firmness and physical stamina. Wright was not someone who would take no for an answer and he would simply keep on going, working as long and hard as required. He also knew how to plan ahead and work toward his objectives, step-by-step. When obstacles arose, he would simply mow them down.

Motivating forces

Wright was a conscientious, hard-working individual. The tall upper zone is a stern taskmaster and reflects strict early parenting. He was the type of person who would do his best, always, not just because it suited or benefited him, but because it was the right thing to do.

Between the lines

Copybook refers to the school model the writer originally learned. Some people continue to adhere to copybook, while others develop their own original forms, either simplifying or elaborating on the school model. Copybook writers such as Wilbur Wright tend to be more comfortable when they stick within set boundaries. They often tend to be attracted to administrative-type careers in nursing, secretarial, and teaching positions.

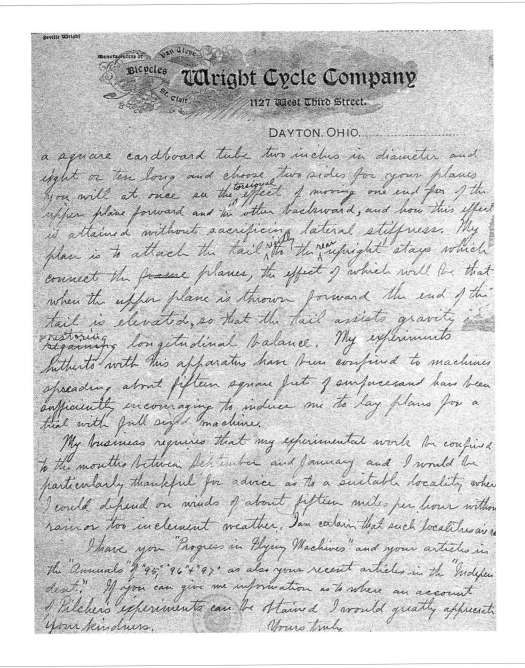

Extract from a letter written by Wilbur Wright, May 13, 1900

... *a square of cardboard tube two inches in diameter and eight or ten long and choose two sides for your planes you will at once see the ... effect of moving one end ... of the upper plane forward and the other backward, and how this effect is attained without sacrificing lateral stiffness. My plan is to attach the tail rigidly ... the rear upright ... which connect the planes, the effect of which will ... that when the upper plane is thrown forward the end of the tail is elevated, so that the tail assists gravity ... longitudinal balance. My experiments hitherto with this apparatus have been confined to machines ... about fifteen square feet of surface and have been sufficiently encouraging to induce me to lay plans for a trial with full sized machines.*

My business requires that my experimental work be confined to the months between September (?) and January and I would be particularly thankful for advice as to a suitable locality where I could depend on winds of about fifteen miles per hour without rain or too ... weather. I am certain that such localities are ...

I have your "Progress in Flying Machines" and your articles in the "Annuals" of "95," "96" & "97" as also your recent articles in the "Independent." If you can give me information as to where an account of Pilcher's (?) experiments can be obtained I would greatly appreciate your kindness.

Yours truly, Wilbur Wright

Glossary

Angular forms
Sharp, straight strokes made by stopping the pen and changing direction before continuing writing.

Arcade forms
Forms that look like arches, rounded on the top and open at the bottom.

Baseline
The invisible line upon which writing rests.

Connectedness
The degree to which one letter attaches to another.

Connective forms
The shape of the connections between letters. Connective forms include garland, arcade, angular, and thread.

Copybook (model)
The standard of handwriting instruction taught in a particular school. Also called school model.

Covering stroke
A stroke that unnecessarily covers over another stroke in a concealing action. *See also* retracing.

Cradle form
Large, round, open strokes on lower-zone letters.

Cursive writing
Writing where one letter is joined to the next.

Double curve
An indefinite connective form that combines the arcade and the garland. Also called a double *s* link, due to its resemblance to the letter *s*.

Downstroke
The movement of the pen toward the writer. The backbone of handwriting, without which the writing becomes completely illegible.

Elaboration
Extra strokes or loops added to a copybook model.

Extremes
Extra length or width, or exaggerated elaboration.

Finals
Final strokes on letters at the end of words.

Form
The writer's chosen writing style (how the writing looks): copybook, elaborated, simplified, or printed.

Form level
The overall appearance of the page. High form level has a pleasing, well-arranged appearance; low form level looks disorganized and unpleasant.

Fullness
The width of the letters compared to copybook, which is a ratio of 1:1 in the middle zone.

Garland form
A cup-like connective form that is open at the top and rounded on the bottom.

Gestalt
A school of handwriting analysis that considers hand-writing as a whole picture made up of spatial arrangement, form, and movement.

Hooks
Tiny, sharp strokes, either on the horizontal or vertical, particularly on *t*-bars and initial or final letters.

Horizontal expansion
The space taken up by 20 characters and spaces.

Impulse pattern
Created by tracing where the writer starts and stops.

Initial stroke
An extra, added stroke at the beginning of a letter.

Knots
Extra loops that appear as if tied in a knot.

Letter space
The amount of space left between letters.

Line space
The amount of space left between lines.

Lower zone
The lower extensions below the baseline such as with the letters *g*, *y*, *j* and *p*.

Margins
The amount of space left around the writing on the page.

Middle zone
The vowel letters and letters without extensions. Every letter passes through the middle zone.

Movement
Writing in four dimensions: up/down; left/right; into the paper; and above the paper (airstrokes).

Muddiness
Heavy, blotchy flow of ink made with heavy pressure.

Natural handwriting
A form achieved once graphic maturity is reached and the writer no longer needs to stop and consciously think about what he or she is writing.

Narrowness
Less than copybook, which is a ratio of 1:1 in the middle zone and 1:0.5 in the upper and lower zones.

Pastosity
A heavy flow of ink but without pressure.

Persona writing
Unnaturally perfect writing that looks as if it were drawn.

Personal pronoun *I*
The capital letter *I*, the single letter in the English language that represents the writer.

Pressure
Grip pressure: how tightly the writer holds the pen.
Primary pressure: the degree to which the pen digs into the paper.
Secondary pressure: the rhythm of light/dark strokes.

Red flags
Warning signs of potential for pathological behavior.

Regularity
A function of rhythm with stronger emphasis on contraction. Highly regular writing looks more mechanical than natural.

Retracing
Upstrokes overlapping downstrokes, particularly where there should be loops.

Rhythm
Forward movement expands (releases) and backward movement contracts. Rhythm is the repeated motion of these patterns of contraction and release.

Shark's teeth
A combination curve/angle that looks like a shark's tooth.

Sharpness
Clean, clear edges of strokes when seen under strong magnification.

Simplification
The elimination of superfluous strokes from the copybook model.

Size
Overall size or the proportions between zones.

Skeletal writing
An extreme form of simplification, where some essential parts are missing.

Slant
The angle of upstrokes and downstrokes in relation to the baseline.

Space
The overall pattern of spatial arrangement on the paper. Includes width of margins, letter, word, and line spacing.

Springboard stroke
An extremely long, straight initial stroke that starts below the baseline.

Speed
The personal pace at which the writer moves the pen across the paper.

Thready form
An indefinite connective form that looks flat and wavy.

Trait stroke
A school of handwriting analysis that assigns personality trait names to individual writing strokes.

Upper zone
The upper extensions on letters such as *l, h* and *b*.

Upstroke
The movement of the pen away from the writer.

Variability
A function of rhythm, with emphasis on release.

Word space
The amount of space left between words.

Zones
The three distinct areas of writing: upper, middle, and lower zones. Each represents a specific area of personality functioning.

Further reading and handwriting organizations

Further reading

Amend, K. K., K. S. Amend and M. S. Ruiz (contributor). *Handwriting Analysis: The Complete Basic Book*. Newcastle Publishing Co., 1986.

Branston, B. *Graphology Explained: A Workbook*. Samuel Weiser, 1991.

The Diagram Group (ed.). *The Little Giant Encyclopedia of Handwriting Analysis*. Sterling Publications, 1999.

Hollander, P.S. *Handwriting Analysis: A Complete Self-Teaching Guide*. Llewellyn Publications, 1998.

Jacoby, H. J. *Analysis of Handwriting*. George Allen & Unwin Ltd, 1938.

Lazewnik, B. M. *Handwriting Analysis: A Guide to Understanding Personalities*. Schiffer Publishing Ltd, 1997.

Lowe, S. *The Complete Idiot's Guide to Handwriting Analysis*. Alpha Books, 1999.

Pulver, M. *The Symbolism of Handwriting*. Scriptor Books, 1994 (translated from the German original 1931 edition).

Roman, K. *Encyclopedia of the Written Word*. Frederick Ungar, 1968.

Roman, K. *Personality in Handwriting*. Pantheon Books, 1952.

Sackheim, K. K. *Handwriting Analysis and the Employee Selection Process: A Guide for Human Resource Professionals*. Quorum Books, 1990.

Saudek, R. *Experiments in Handwriting*. Books for Professionals, 1978.
_____. *The Psychology of Handwriting*. Books for Professionals, 1978.

Sonnemann, U. *The Psychology of Handwriting*. Grune & Stratton, 1950.

Teillard, A. *The Soul and Handwriting*. Scriptor Books, 1993.

Victor, F. *Handwriting: A Personality Projection*. Fern Ridge Press, 1989.

Wolff, W. *Diagrams of the Unconscious*. Grune & Stratton, 1948.

Recommended handwriting analysis organizations in the United States

These educational groups welcome anyone who is interested in handwriting. Most offer newsletters, conferences, and certification testing.

The Vanguard Network for Handwriting Professionals and Serious Students
The Vanguard is not a formal organization. It is a network of ethical handwriting professionals and serious students actively pursuing a career in handwriting analysis. The Vanguard offers a quarterly periodical, seminars, and conferences. Information about events, a certification syllabus, and a free copy of the Vanguard newsletter are available for downloading from <<*http://www.writinganalysis.com*>>. A free demonstration of Sheila Lowe's Handwriting Analyzer, an award-winning computer program designed to provide accurate personality assessment, can also be downloaded from this site. Or you may contact Sheila Lowe directly by phone at (661) 259-8979 or e-mail her at *writechoice@prodigy.net*

American Handwriting Analysis Foundation
P.O. Box
San Jose, CA 95150
tel: (800) 826-7774
e-mail: *ahaf@tucson.com*
<<*http://www.tucson.com/handwriting*>>

American Association of Handwriting Analysts
P.O. Box 3087
Southfield, MI 48037-3087
tel: (248) 746-0740
e-mail: *AAHAOffice@aol.com*

National Society for Graphology
250 W. 57th St., Suite 1228A
New York, NY 10108
tel: (212) 265-1148

American Society of Professional Graphologists
2025 Kings Highway
Brooklyn, NY 11229
tel: (718) 339-6868

Handwriting Analysis Research Library
Robert E. Backman, Curator
91, Washington St.
Greenfield, MA 01301-3411
tel: (413) 774-4667

Overseas handwriting analysis organizations

The following are foreign organizations or recommended individuals to contact for information about graphology.

Belgian Graphologists' Association
67, Rue de la Allee
1050 Brussels, Belgium

Graziella Pettinati
3330, Chemin Ste. Foy
Ste. Foy, QC, Canada GIX 1Z8
e-mail: *graffiti@acica.com*

Finland
<<*http://www.kolumbus.fi/grafologinen.yhdistys/*>>

Groupement des Graphologues Conseils de France
c/o Monique Riley
49, rue Ste. Radegonde
78100 St. Germain-en-Laye, France

Helmut Ploog
Rossinistreet 9

D-85598 Baldham
Near Munich, Germany
e-mail: *dr.ploog@t-online.de*

Fausto Brugnatelli
Milan, Italy
e-mail: *brgcons@tiscalinet.it*

Gaetano Rizzo
Italian list: *la_scrittura@yahoogroups.com*

Dutch Graphological Society
Postbus 918
3160 AC Rhoon, The Netherlands
e-mail: *maresi.de.monchy@wxs.nl*

Maria-Victoria Sen Samaranch
Paseo Bonanova 17
08022 Barcelona, Spain

Switzerland
<<*http://www.sgg-graphologie.ch*>>

The British Academy of Graphology
Administrative Centre
11, Roundacre
London SW19 6DB, United Kingdom
Web site: <<*http://www.graphology.co.uk*>>

The Graphology Information Center
<<*http://www.graphology.ws*>>

Nigel Bradley
e-mail: *bradlen@westminster.ac.uk*

Picture credits

AKG London: 27, 41, 45, 59, 71, 113, 120; Associated Press: 48, 67, 135, 139; The British Library: 7, 83, 153; Brown Partworks: National Archives: 92; Andrew Carnegie Birthplace Museum: 23; Charles Chaplin Estate: 29; Christie's Images: 79, 87, 93, 141, 147; Churchill Archives Centre, Churchill College: 31; Williams Clark Library, University of California: 151; Corbis: 25, 66, 96, 116 Bettmann: 12, 14, 46, 52, 56, 78, 86, 102, 109, 115, 128, 136; Francis G. Mayer: 146; Matthew Mendleson: 34; Reuters Newsmedia Inc.: 18, S.I.N: 36; Gavin Wickham/Eye Ubiquitous: 138; James Dean Memorial Gallery: 47; Dickens House: 51; Edison National Historic Site: 57; Mary Evans Picture Library: 61, 119, 145; William Faulkner Collection, University of Virginia: 65; Hargrett Rare Book and Manuscript Library, University of Georgia Libraries: 105; Joe Hiles: 13; by permission of the Houghton Library: 53; Hulton Getty: 8, 10, 16, 20, 21, 22, 26, 28, 38, 39, 40, 42, 44, 50, 54, 58, 60, 64, 68, 70, 72, 74, 76, 80, 94, 104, 106, 110, 118, 124, 126, 132, 134, 140, 142, 148, 150, 152, 154; Imperial War Museum: 85; International Women's Air and Space Museum: 55; John Fitzgerald Kennedy Library: 91; Lebrecht Collection: 9, 11, 111; Library of Congress: 69, 77, 149, 155; National Archives: 107, 123; National Museum of American History, Smithsonian Institute: 63; Novosti London: 137; Patton Society: 117; Pearce Civil War Documents Collection: 43, 75, 99; Pictorial Press: 81; Pollock-Krasner House: 121; Robert Hunt Library: 6, 24, 30, 62, 82, 84, 88, 90, 98, 108, 112, 114, 122, 130, 144; Rockefeller Archive Centre: 127; Roger-Viollet: 101; Franklin D. Roosevelt Library: 129, 131; Scott Polar Research Institute: 133; Topham: 95, 103.

Between the lines

Angles - Louis XIV (p.100)

Baseline - Thomas Jefferson (p.86)

Baseline (concave) - Galileo Galilei (p.72)

Baseline (upward slant) - Donald Trump (p.142)

Capitals - Henry VIII (p.82)

Connective forms - James Dean (p.46)

Connectedness - Thomas Edison (p.56)

Contraction/release - Abraham Lincoln (p.98)

Copybook - Wilbur Wright (p.154)

Covering stokes (on *a*) - Kurt Cobain (p.36)

Cradle lower zone - Princess Diana (p.48)

Elaboration - John Hancock (p.76)

Extremes - William Faulkner (p.64)

Finals - John D. Rockefeller (p.126)

Form level - Jacqueline Kennedy Onassis (p.88)

Fullness/narrowness - George Bush Jr. (p.18)

Garlands - Amelia Earhart (p.54)

Gender - Eleanor Roosevelt (p.128)

Gestalt - Virginia Woolf (p.152)

Greek letters - Jackson Pollock (p.120)

Hooks - Ludwig van Beethoven (p.10)

Horizontal expansion - Queen Victoria (p.144)

Ideal sample - Marilyn Monroe (p.108)

i-dots - Johann Sebastian Bach (p.8)

Illegibility - Charles Darwin (p.44)

Impulse patterns - James Whistler (p.148)

Initial strokes - David Berkowitz (p.12)

Initial strokes - Ted Bundy (p.14)

Knots and ties - Napoleon Bonaparte (p.112)

Letter *d* - Benjamin Franklin (p.68)

Letter *f* - James Monroe (p.106)

Letter *k* - Ulysses S. Grant (p.74)

Letter space - John F. Kennedy (p.90)

Letter *t* - Charlie Chaplin (p.28)

Limitations of handwriting analysis - Catherine the Great (p.26)

Line spacing - Elizabeth I (p.60)

Linear writing - Robert E. Lee (p.92)

Lower zone - Jane Austen (p.6)

Margins - George Washington (p.146)

Middle zone - Ronald Reagan (p.124)

Middle-zone size - Mother Teresa (p.138)

Mirror writing - Leonardo da Vinci (p.96)

Muddiness - Adolf Hitler (p.84)

Nationality - Marie Curie (p.40)

Natural writing - Christopher Columbus (p.38)

Organization - Winston Churchill (p.30)

Pastosity - Wolfgang Amadeus Mozart (p.110)

Persona writing - F. Scott Fitzgerald (p.66)

Personal pronoun *I* - Franklin D. Roosevelt (p.130)

Pressure - Jimi Hendrix (p.80)

Pressure in photocopies - Ernest Shackleton (p. 132)

Printing - John Lennon (p.94)

Red flags - Lee Harvey Oswald (p.114)

Regularity - Andrew Carnegie (p.22)

Retracing - George Custer (p.42)

Rhythm - Hillary Clinton (p.34)

Rhythm (released) - Duke Ellington (p.62)

Rivers - Lord Byron (p.20)

Rolled-in strokes - Emily Dickinson (p.52)

Signature - Charles Dickens (p.50)

Simplification - Paul McCartney (p.102)

Shark's teeth - Joseph Stalin (p.136)

Slant - Ernest Hemingway (p.78)

Small size - Dylan Thomas (p.140)

Speed - Albert Einstein (p.58)

Thread - George Patton (p.116)

Tics (lower zone) - George Bush Sr. (p.16)

Trait stroke - Fidel Castro (p.24)

Upper-zone elaboration - Elvis Presley (p.122)

Upper-zone height - Bill Clinton (p.32)

Variability - O.J. Simpson (p.134)

Writing in relief - Margaret Mitchell (p.104)

Word space - Oscar Wilde (p.150)

Zonal proportions - Edgar Allan Poe (p.118)

Zones - Sigmund Freud (p.70)